Also by Nicky Hayes

Foundations of Psychology
Doing Psychological Research
Teach Yourself Psychology
Teach Yourself Applied Psychology
Successful Team Management

Psychology in Perspective

Second Edition

Nicky Hayes

palgrave

First edition 1995
Reprinted twice
Second edition 2002

Published by
PALGRAVE
Houndmills, Basingstoke, Hampshire RG21 6XS and 175 Fifth Avenue,
New York, N.Y. 10010
Companies and representatives throughout the world

PALGRAVE is the new global academic imprint of St. Martin's Press
LLC Scholarly and Reference Division and Palgrave Publishers Ltd
(formerly Macmillan Press Ltd).

ISBN 0–333–98396–3 hardback
ISBN 0–333–96022–X paperback

This book is printed on paper suitable for recycling and made from fully
managed and sustained forest sources.

A catalogue record for this book is available from the British Library.

Library of Congress Cataloging-in-Publication Data

Hayes, Nicky.
    Psychology in perspective / Nicky Hayes. – 2nd ed.
        p. cm.
    Includes bibliographical references and index.
    ISBN 0–333–98396–3
        1. Psychology. I. Title.

BF121 .H28 2002
150 – dc21   2001036981

10   9   8   7   6   5   4   3   2   1
11 10 09 08 07 06 05 04 03 02

Printed in China

Coventry University

To Chris Lenton

Contents

List of Figures

Preface

Science is not value-free. It exists in society, and it reflects society's assumptions. Research funding, scientific publication and the scientific community's decisions about what counts as valid knowledge all reflect the social contexts in which they take place. As society changes, so too do the interests and emphases of scientific research.

Psychology is not exempt from these processes. Like the other sciences, psychology exists in a social context – or a variety of social contexts – and its concerns are also those of the wider society within which it is located. Psychology's internal development – its theories, its evidence and its subject matter – all mirror those concerns. They also contribute to them, both directly and indirectly.

That doesn't mean, however, that either psychology or other scientific disciplines follow every fad and fashion in society. Change takes time, and it rarely happens as a complete upheaval. Instead, it occurs in a much more piecemeal fashion, as new movements or ideas gather momentum. It is six years since the first edition of *Psychology in Perspective* was published, and the changes which have become apparent in psychology since that time are not totally new. They were detectable then. But during the intervening years, they have become stronger and more clearly delineated.

For example, qualitative methodologies as valid aspects of psychological research have become far more broadly accepted than they were six years ago. Discourse analysis has become effectively a part of the psychological establishment, and those who were once seen as being 'on the fringe' are now respected professors in well-established psychology departments. Qualitative research reports have been appearing in 'mainstream' psychology journals, and qualitative techniques are being used to supplement quantitative methods across the whole of the discipline. What was seen in 1991 as a radical challenge for psychology (so much so that the British Psychological Society set up a working party to look into it) has become gradually accepted as an enrichment of its methodology.

These changes didn't happen overnight. They came about because of the hard work of a number of dedicated academics.

Their efforts meant that the value of qualitative methods became more widely recognised, and anxieties about academic rigour were explicitly addressed. Moreover, the new approach fitted with an increasing recognition of the limitations of conventional methodologies, and a wider social as well as academic recognition of the importance of human experiences and values.

Psychology never stays the same – there are always new areas opening up, and other areas fading into the background. But sometimes, we find old wine in new bottles, to misphrase the cliché. What seems to be a new development is simply more of the same type of argument, given a different name. The branch of psychology known as evolutionary psychology, for example, has announced itself as a new area of the discipline, but it bears an uncanny resemblance to its forebears – in the recent past sociobiology, and before that the genetic determinism of Lorenz and Morris. Their arguments are much the same – not identical, of course, but much the same; and the counter-arguments haven't changed all that much either.

In this second edition of *Psychology in Perspective*, the original ten essays of the first edition have been brought up to date and, sometimes, expanded. They have also been augmented by four new ones, creating a set of discussions which range across the psychological discipline, encompassing philosophical theories, schools of thought, social movements and human potential.

This broad-ranging overview of psychological issues is, inevitably, a selection rather than a comprehensive discussion. But I hope that you will find it a stimulating one. It raises issues about the adequacy of research and evidence, about the social contexts within which research is located, and about the social responsibility of science. Psychological theorising often has political and socio-political implications which range far beyond the intentions of the original researchers. We need to be aware of these implications, in the same way that we need to be aware of our history, if we are to develop a true understanding of why modern psychology is like it is.

NICKY HAYES

Chapter 1

Reductionism in Psychological Theory

One of the biggest problems in psychology's quest to understand the human being has been our tendency to fall back on reductionism as a means of explaining why human beings are like they are. Reductionism is a way of going about explanation. When we talk of reductionist theories, we are referring to a set of ideas which have one distinguishing characteristic – the belief that things can be explained simply by reducing them down to their constituent parts. In other words, reductionist arguments state that things can be understood as being nothing but the sum of their components.

The philosophical background of reductionism can be found in the theory put forward by Descartes (1596–1650), in the seventeenth century. Descartes's approach is often known as Cartesian dualism, because he was making distinctions between two phenomena: the human mind, with its capacity to reason; and animal nature, which he saw as mechanistic and instinctive, and in which he included the human body. He regarded these as two separate things, which is why his theory is referred to as dualist.

In describing the mind–body distinction, Descartes argued that the mind was a completely different, separate entity from the body. The body, he believed, was purely a machine, operating like a machine and not influencing the mind at all. The mind, on the other hand, was the seat of reason and the essence of being human – hence Descartes's famous definition of what it was to be human: 'I think, therefore I am.' Descartes went on to argue that the distinction between mind and body made human beings fundamentally different from animals, in that animal behaviour was mechanistic (machine-like) and unthinking, operating from instincts rather than from reasoning; whereas humans were able to think and to use language, which made them distinctively human.

Although this may not seem to be particularly relevant, it is important for understanding reductionism in psychology, for several reasons. For one thing, Descartes had produced what became the first explanation of the mind without reference to religious argument in the Europe of that time. This happened just when European thinking was just breaking free from the domination of medieval theology, so as a philosophical principle it formed the basis for investigations into the nature of the mind, which eventually developed into 'experimental philosophy' and later 'psychology'. Descartes's emphasis on instincts and his view of the body as a machine established a tradition in European psychological thinking which has continued up to the present day.

Secondly, his idea of the body as a machine not only legitimised its use in the growing factories of the Industrial Revolution (one reason why his ideas became so popular); but also formed the basis of modern medicine. The disputes between supporters of holistic medicine (which treats the body and the mind as inseparable) and those of traditional medicine (which sees the body as a machine, working independently from the mind) are a direct legacy from Descartes. Modern medicine's allegiance to the idea of the body as a machine is perhaps expressed most clearly in its emphasis on spare-part surgery; while practitioners of holistic medicine emphasise treatments which will encourage the body's own restorative powers to come into effect.

Thirdly, perceiving both the human body and animal behaviour as mechanistic implied that each of them could be studied in terms of their component parts, in much the same way as we might study a car engine by looking at the parts which it contains. So, for instance, you read in Richard Gregory's popular book *Eye and Brain* about Descartes dissecting an ox eye and, on seeing the upside-down image on the retina, concluding that the eye acts like a camera, producing an image which is later processed and analysed. Many theories in physiological psychology have started from this kind of approach, using machine-like models to try to understand what is happening. And most of these also have had to be seriously revised, as researchers gain a better understanding of the human processes underlying them.

Descartes, then, could justifiably be called one of the first reductionists, in that his reduction of the human body to a machine, and of animal behaviour to mechanical, instinctive operations, adopts that form of argument. In so doing, he established a style of reasoning about the human mind which is still very much alive and kicking in psychology.

There are three particularly striking examples of reductionist theories which most people encounter when they first learn about psychology. These are behaviourism, neurological reductionism, and genetic determinism. There are other forms of reductionism too, most notably social reductionism. Each of these has its problems, which we will look at briefly before going on to look at some more general issues raised by reductionist argument.

Behaviourism

The behaviourist revolution at the beginning of the twentieth century centred around J. B. Watson's attempt to make psychology 'scientific'. Where, previously, psychology had concentrated on the study of the mind, Watson (1913) argued that the 'mind' was not suitable for valid scientific research, because it could only be examined subjectively. He argued that the only truly scientific approach for psychology was to keep to the study of things which could be objectively observed. In the case of living 'organisms', as he put it, that meant studying behaviour, because that is the only evidence that we can examine directly. It isn't possible to know for certain what someone is thinking, but we can use their behaviour as a guide. If they smile and nod, for example, we can judge that they agree with what we are saying, even though we can't see directly into the mind.

Watson's attempt to make psychology scientific involved modelling it on the other sciences, by which he meant physics, chemistry and biology. Those sciences, interestingly enough, had all had developments which had occurred at least in the previous century, which had transformed them completely, and greatly increased their explanatory powers. Watson considered that a scientific psychology would also undergo such a transformation; and it was on this that he modelled his view of scientific psychology.

The particular development which had occurred in physics was the development of atomic theory. Not the Einstein version, leading to atom bombs and power; but the original idea that matter consists of atoms, which combine together to form molecules. Once this idea had been established, physical phenomena such as heat and structure could be explained in very much more meaningful terms. A similar development in chemistry dealt with the relationship between different forms of matter. The concept of valency and the development of the periodic table of the elements meant that chemistry became unified as a science, and could make sense out of many more of its established observations.

In biology, two significant developments served to unify the discipline. One was cell theory: the discovery that all living things were constructed of small units – living cells. For the first time, this provided a biological link between plants and animals, which meant that all sorts of things which didn't previously make sense started to show connections, and biology was finally established as a 'true' science. The other major development in biology was Mendelian genetics – still very much a talking point in Watson's day, but demonstrating how it was possible to perceive inheritance in terms of small units of heredity with definite principles of combination, and making sense out of evolutionary theory.

All of these developments have two things in common. Firstly, the discovery of small constituent units had developed and unified each of the disciplines concerned. Secondly, they had all occurred or become widely known in the previous century; and so the impact that they had had on their respective disciplines was well-known. When Watson was looking to build a scientific psychology, it was to the sciences that he looked; and when he looked to the sciences he saw the identification of small 'building blocks' as being of crucial importance in scientific development.

It is important to remember that this definition of the nature of science by Watson is different from the definition of science that was held by the 'introspectionist' psychologists. Watson was defining a science largely in terms of its subject matter, and in particular whether it had managed to identify the basic units in its area of study. The introspectionists, however, defined science in terms of the methods of investigation which were being used. Psychologists such as Wilhelm Wundt, William James and Herman Ebbinghaus had been extremely concerned to go about their studies in a scientific manner, using rigorous methodology. But their subject matter – the human mind – was in Watson's eyes inherently unscientific.

Watson identified stimulus–response (S–R) connections as the basic units of psychology. A complete understanding of behaviour, he considered, could be built up from the systematic study of S–R connections and how they combined. He emphasised the study of learning as the basis of psychology, because that was the way that stimulus–response links were established; and he studied animal learning because, he believed, it represented a relatively 'pure' form of stimulus–response link, uncontaminated by as much previous learning and memory as it would be in human beings. His reasoning was that if S–R links were the basic foundation of behaviour, then all S–R links would be similar in essence, in much the same way as different atoms or cells are similar in essence, even though specific details may vary.

Behaviourism, of course, wasn't the only approach in psychology at that time. A strong challenge to the reductionism of the behaviourist school was put forward by the Gestalt psychologists in Europe. They argued that many aspects of human behaviour could not realistically be seen as combinations of stimulus– response connections, but were much more than just the sum of their parts. They devoted considerable research efforts to studying aspects of human experience which could not be broken down in this way – most notably perceptual organisation and problem-solving.

For example: the tendency of individuals to organise their perception into figures against backgrounds, rather than seeing a disconnected pattern of light and dark patches, seems to be one of the earliest perceptual skills. Even very young infants respond selectively to patterned stimuli, and they respond very strongly indeed to patterns bearing resemblances to human faces. Without some inherent organisation of sensory impressions into figures and backgrounds, distinguishing faces from anything else would be impossible. And a purely empirical approach entirely based on S–R associations, such as was presented by the early behaviourists, is completely inadequate to explain such phenomena.

An even more convincing example is given in the case of the Necker cube (Figure 1.1) where exactly the same stimulus presented to the retina produces two different experiences. Any attempt to explain this in terms of learned associations comes to grief on the fact that the stimulus is identical, even when it is being perceived in different ways. Further work with ambiguous stimuli, such as those used by Leeper in 1935 (Figure 1.2), highlighted such factors as the importance of 'set' in perception, and behaviourist attempts to explain perceptual organisation receded more and more into the background.

Similarly, research into insight learning by Köhler in 1925 demonstrated what seemed to be much more holistic forms of learning than those which could be produced by S–R training. Insight learning seemed to take place by a sudden cognitive (mental)

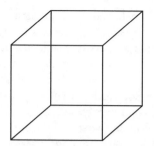

FIGURE 1.1   The Necker cube

restructuring of the whole problem, leading to rapid problem-solving instead of trial-and-error attempts. Although Harlow (1949) did show that enough experience of trial-and-error learning with similar problems could produce what looked like insight, it was clear that some aspects of insight didn't seem to be a simple matter of learning sets. The work on insight learning was taken up in studies of human problem-solving, and again the simple behaviourist explanations became inadequate and receded into the background.

FIGURE 1.2   The 'rat-man' figure

Perhaps the most important discovery of the Gestalt psychologists, though, in terms of their arguments against reductionism, was the principle of closure. This demonstrated the human tendency to go far beyond the data, to combine incomplete images or sounds into whole pictures or meaningful units. The various examples of the principles of closure showed that in many instances S–R explanations just didn't make any sense at all. Often, the information that a human being receives as the stimulus is completely inadequate for piecing together by learned association, yet we manage to make sense out of it. For example, when we see a set of moving dots which have been attached to someone's shoulder, knee and elbow joints, we have no difficulty seeing a complete person. Mentally, we 'close up' the dots to form a complete image. We do the same when we see cartoons of faces, yet the difficulty of programming computers to do tasks like face recognition has shown just what a complex cognitive event it is. People do it easily, but not, it seems, through trial and error.

We can see, then, that although some aspects of behaviour may be explicable in S–R terms, others are very much harder to explain. The modern-day 'neo-behaviourists' have largely dropped the reductionist approach adopted by Watson, and some of them argue instead for an 'interactionist' perspective, in which cognition and environmental learning are seen to be working together to produce particular behaviours. Their emphasis is still on behaviour and S–R links, but they no longer consider that to be the only possible level of explanation in psychology. We will be looking at behaviourism in more detail in Chapter 2, but for now we will move on to consider another major source of reductionism: neurological reductionism.

Neurological reductionism

Descartes's view of the human body as a machine led to an emphasis in medical practice on illness as occurring when some mechanism or part had gone 'wrong' with it. This idea has been applied not only to physical illness, but also in the cases of people who show peculiar or disturbing social behaviour patterns – that is, the kind of behaviour which we now refer to as 'mental illness'. The medical model of mental illness, which is largely (though not completely) accepted in Western society, sees abnormal behaviour as being 'caused' by something going wrong with the machinery of the mind – the neurones or chemicals which underlie mental functioning. One version of this is known as neurological reductionism.

Neurological reductionism can be seen most clearly in the medical approach to schizophrenia – a disturbance in which people often speak irrationally, and seem to hold peculiar beliefs which are not in tune with their objective reality. Schizophrenics often show other forms of peculiar behaviour too, such as catatonia, in which the person seems to 'lock' into a trance, and the body remains rigid for a long period of time – sometimes several hours.

Medical research has shown that schizophrenics have certain imbalances of brain chemicals; and this is taken by some members of the medical profession as 'proof' that the disorder is 'caused' by those chemicals. If we take the simple view that the chemicals in the brain cause all of our thinking, then that would appear to be a straightforward logical conclusion. But if we remember that a single anxious thought, such as suddenly remembering something which we find disturbing, stimulates the production of a different set of brain chemicals and a complete physiological reaction in the body, then that conclusion starts to look a little too simple.

Kallman's (1938) twin studies, appeared to show that schizophrenia or a 'schizoid' tendency could run in families. This was taken as implying that it was inherited; but Kallman used a very loose definition of 'schizoid', such that just about any kind of unusual behaviour could count. Moreover, the clinical judgements were also made by Kallman himself (sometimes without even seeing the people concerned), who knew all the details and intentions of the study, and believed firmly in the idea of genetic influence. It is obvious how vulnerable this way of doing things is to unconscious bias, even in a researcher with the best of motives. Nowadays, we would insist on far better controls in such a study.

More modern research also shows a link between families and schizophrenia (although not nearly as strong as Kallman's); but just because something runs in families doesn't make it genetic. Families also pass on culture, habits and explanations to one another; and they socialise their children into ways of reacting to stressors as well as into ways of behaving with other people.

Laing (1965) argued that the disorder of schizophrenia could be produced by intolerable social demands. As early as the 1950s, Bateson *et al.* put forward the 'double-bind' theory of schizophrenia, which showed how the families of schizophrenics often trapped those people in situations where just about anything they did would produce censure and hostility from other family members. The situation where a teenager is told 'You're never at home nowadays', but on staying in receives the complaint of 'Can't we ever get any peace and quiet without you hanging about all the time', is an everyday example of the sort of thing that Bateson meant – although Bateson was really talking about much more extreme examples.

Following on from this, the psychiatrist R. D. Laing (1965) showed how the apparently irrational symptoms shown by schizophrenics often mirrored the conflicts which they were encountering. A case study given in *Sanity, Madness and the Family* by Laing and

Esterson (1968) is of a girl whose delusion was that she imagined herself trapped in a perpetual game of tennis, as the tennis ball in play. On investigating her family situation, Laing found that the family had a deep rift, with the mother and her mother's father on one side, and the father and his mother forming the other side. The girl was obliged to act as go-between between the two sides of the family, including carrying hostile and emotional messages which distressed her deeply. Eventually she was unable to cope with this any further, and became catatonic – rigid and unable to move.

Laing and Esterson were pointing out how the apparently irrational symptoms of schizophrenia could be seen to make sense, if they were taken in the context of the person's actual existence in the world. In this case, although the girl herself, on a conscious level, did not understand what was happening to her, on a subconscious level her symptoms were reflecting the double-bind that she found herself in. Everything she did was judged as wrong, and so by becoming catatonic, she 'froze', and didn't do anything at all. And the schizophrenic fugue of the tennis game reflected her role within the family.

Laing showed how schizophrenics often came from deeply disturbed families, which he called 'schizophregenic' (likely to bring about schizophrenia in their members). These generally had considerable amounts of suppressed conflict and double-binds in their everyday interaction, and the schizophrenic person was too sensitive to be able to cope with these. He also showed how the presence of someone who could be seen by the family as 'ill' was used and perpetuated by the family. It allowed them to focus the family disturbance around that person and so to distract attention from their other disturbed relationships. The 'sick' individual, in other words, became the scapegoat for the whole family.

The point is this: a complex phenomenon like schizophrenia is not 'explained' simply by talking about chemicals in the brain. That the chemicals exist is indisputable. That altering the level of chemicals through drugs can suppress symptoms is also not disputed – although it is questionable how far suppressing symptoms is the same as curing them. But to argue from there that the chemicals 'cause' schizophrenia is to neglect all the other levels of explanation which may be needed in order to understand fully what is going on.

Laing may have taken his case to extremes, but we cannot ignore the existence of family disturbance as an additional factor in schizophrenia. Indeed, thanks to Laing's work, many professionals now use what has become known as the 'vulnerability' model of schizophrenia – the idea that some people may be vulnerable to schizophrenia, perhaps for neurological reasons, but that they will only develop the problem if they are placed under intolerable stresses. Otherwise, they will be fine, and live their lives as normally as anyone else.

There are other examples of the way in which simple neurological reductionism is inadequate to explain what is going on. One of them is the role of motivation in recovery from cerebral strokes. If we adopt a mechanistic approach to brain functioning, then if parts of the brain become damaged as a result of an interruption to the blood supply, we would expect that damage to remain. But that isn't how it works. The reality is that patients who are highly motivated and try very hard to overcome the problems will often recover almost complete functioning, while those who accept their condition passively remain crippled or paralysed. Their own beliefs affect how much effort they make to recover, and that in turn affects how much they do recover.

Similarly, Parkinson's disease is considered to result from a deficiency in the amount of the chemical dopamine in the brain. Patients with Parkinson's disease find coordinated physical action extremely difficult, if not impossible. Yet faced with an emergency, like nearly being run over when crossing a road, they can react very quickly. The comedian Terry-Thomas, who suffered from Parkinsonism later in his life, described how at one time he found himself unable to *walk* through the door of his bedroom. Yet, when he tried, he found that he could *dance* through it. The extra effort and determination needed to do something as difficult as dancing enabled him to overcome the effects of the brain disease, at least temporarily. These findings are very hard to explain if Parkinsonism is simply seen as a collection of symptoms which are 'caused' by dopamine deficiency in the brain.

The fact is that there is a continuous interaction between people's beliefs and cognitions, the brain, the environment that they are in, and their behaviour. To take just one example, the brain will react to certain environmental situations – like, say, particularly threatening ones – by the production of specific chemicals; these chemicals in turn can influence our physical reaction to the environment, by providing us with more energy; and both of them influence how we comprehend what is actually happening. They all interact continuously. To argue that the chemicals 'cause' the behaviour is to take a very simplistic and narrow view of what is happening, which ignores the rest of the picture. We need explanations which can take more than one aspect of a problem into account – which can deal with different levels of explanation.

Genetic determinism

Genetic determinism in psychology has manifest itself in many different ways. I do not intend to deal with one of the most contentious issues here – that of innate intelligence – because that is dealt with elsewhere in this book (see Chapter 12). And we will be looking at some of the specifically human-related examples of genetic determinism in more detail in Chapter 3. So here, I shall concentrate on a different aspect of genetic determinism: the global accounts of inherited behaviour which have emerged from ethological studies of animals.

Research into animal behaviour has always invited theories about human beings, ever since Darwin first published the theory of evolution. Although the history of these ideas makes fascinating reading, here we will just concentrate on ideas in the second half of the twentieth century. In the 1950s and 1960s, writers such as Konrad Lorenz and Desmond Morris argued that because certain forms of behaviour occurred in certain animals, and because human beings were also animals in evolutionary terms, then similar behaviours shown by human beings were genetic and inevitable.

Interestingly enough, these writers tended to ignore the vast range of diversity in behaviour shown by different species of animals, as well as the flexibility of behaviour shown by primates – those species closest to human beings. Instead, they focused particularly on just one or two species (usually birds or fish). Interestingly too, their focus was always on the 'darker' side of animal behaviour, so we had endearing qualities such as aggression, territoriality and xenophobia 'explained' as part of our inescapable biological heritage, and something which we could do nothing about. They were caused by genetic influences and that was that.

In more recent days these theories have taken on a new turn, through a version of evolutionary theory which proved able to explain even such things as people being nice to one another as if it were basically 'selfish' or unpleasant. The new version, known as sociobiology, was put forward by E. O. Wilson in 1975, in his book *Sociobiology*; and it was made accessible to the general public by Richard Dawkins, in *The Selfish Gene* and his various follow-up books. Altruistic or helping behaviour had largely been ignored by Lorenz and Morris, mainly because it was difficult to see how this showed the darker side of human nature. But the new concept of kin selection meant that this could actually be explained as a selfish act, and so that made it all right.

Wilson argued that it is all about saving relatives: if an individual were to lay down its life for an individual who shared its genes, then its line would be perpetuated even though its own life wasn't. He, and Dawkins, went on from there to argue that all animals, including human beings, were simply products of their 'selfish genes', and that to think otherwise was purely an illusion. Society – and particularly the darker side of it – is as it is because this is an inevitable result of the selfish gene.

What is important about this theory isn't so much the merits or demerits of its application in understanding the behaviour of white ants or bumble bees, in the study of which the ideas were first formulated. The problems lie in its application to human behaviour. Reducing human behaviour down to the action of individual 'genes' means that sociobiologists ignore a whole range of other influences on human behaviour, which in many cases are crucially important to understanding people.

There is a more detailed discussion of sociobiology and its weaknesses in Chapter 13, but the most important point here is the way that this approach to understanding human beings focuses on just one level of explanation. In doing so, it ignores all of the other levels of explanation which we need to use to understand why people are like they are.

In order to understand this point, we need to look at how sociobiologists argue their cases. Broadly speaking, this consists of three stages: (1) identifying some kind of 'universal' in behaviour; (2) postulating some kind of 'gene' which could account for the behaviour's existence; and (3) seeking a plausible, evolutionary argument of how that behaviour 'must' have evolved. From then on, any alternative explanation is completely ignored.

There are many other weaknesses in this procedure, which we will look at in more detail in Chapter 13. But, in essence, as Gould (1981) pointed out, by looking for separate explanations for each particular behaviour, sociobiologists act in the same way as if Galileo had looked for separate explanations for each of the weights, feather and cannonballs that he supposedly (but apparently mythically) dropped off the Leaning Tower of Pisa. Rather than trying to explain the feather's behaviour by postulating some property of 'featherness', and the cannon ball's behaviour by postulating 'cannonballness', Galileo identified two physical rules – friction and gravity – which between them can explain a whole range of behaviours.

Similarly, if we look for the underlying rules within the biological potential of the human being, we find a whole range of possible human behaviours, not just a few limited options. It makes no sense to talk of human beings as innately aggressive on the grounds that even currently peaceful societies have had aggressive events in their past; because that doesn't allow us to explain their currently peaceful behaviour. Rather, we need to talk of human beings as having the potential for either aggression or peacefulness, and a whole range of behaviours in between (Gould, 1981).

Which brings me on to the main problem of genetic reductionism: its way of focusing on all the most negative attributes of human behaviour; and arguing that these are inevitable because they are biologically determined. Other attributes – such as the peaceable behaviour in the previous example – could be equally well defended but are somehow never selected. And this shows very clearly the political and social nature of these theories. By presenting a static view of the individual, and stating that it is futile to try to change it, these ideas serve to defend and to legitimise all sorts of repressive social practices. After all, they are simply keeping our nasty biological natures in check, aren't they?

Social reductionism

Another common form of reductionism in psychology is less obviously political than the previous example, but still serves to distract attention away from questions about power and control in society. That is the idea of social reductionism. Although we will be looking at perspectives in social psychology in more detail in Chapters 6 and 7, it is worth outlining the main issues here. Essentially, social reductionism is the attempt to explain what happens in society simply in terms of the individual qualities of particular people.

The clearest examples of this come with research into social prejudice. Much of this research arose as a result of what happened in Germany before and during the Second World War, when Jews, Gypsies and other groups of people were first segregated from the rest of German society, and then systematically murdered, in huge numbers, in the death camps. Although the camps themselves were kept relatively quiet, there were over 200 of them in Germany alone, and the whole process of what was referred to as the 'Final Solution' was widely known and discussed. The holocaust happened against a background of widespread and accepted racial prejudice and discrimination – not just in Germany, but throughout Europe.

That was a social phenomenon, but the attempts by psychologists to understand racism and social prejudice during the decades which followed mostly took an individualistic approach. For example, Adorno *et al.* (1950) attempted to explain social prejudice in terms of the 'authoritarian personality', looking for aspects of personality which would lead to rigidity and intolerance in the person's thinking, and so produce social prejudice. Adorno successfully showed that such a personality syndrome existed, and could explain why some people are more likely to be prejudiced than others. But this couldn't account for why a whole society had connived in the Final Solution, and it completely ignored the wider sociological and economic issues which were also involved. It may have been one part of the answer, but it certainly wasn't the whole story.

At the Nuremberg trials, after the war, the most common defence of those Nazis involved in the atrocities was that they were only obeying orders. Milgram conducted an impressive series of experiments showing that even ordinary people could obey orders to the point of actually killing someone. But when he tried to explain why this happened, Milgram too avoided issues of social power and influence, and explained it in terms of individual states of being (Milgram, 1973). Again, his work provided part of an answer, but not all of it.

There are other examples of social reductionism too, such as Philip Zimbardo's attempt to explain crowd behaviour in terms of deindividuation, which ignores the very real social inequalities which underlie riots – and also fails to explain responsible behaviour by peaceful crowds. Similarly, Bibb Latané's social impact theory explains bystander intervention or apathy purely in terms of the numbers of individuals concerned, entirely ignoring questions of social belief and social structure.

The point is this: that accounting for social events in terms of the actions and ideas of individuals is not enough. There are other factors involved as well. As Tajfel (1981) showed in his studies of group behaviour, there are real differences in power and control between different groups in society, and these influence how individual people act and think. We can't ignore these other levels, even though we may choose to focus on just one aspect of human behaviour for research purposes. The explanations and theories that we develop need to link with these other levels and work with them, not simply ignore their existence.

Reductionism as a general approach

The real problem with reductionism, though, is that as a way of looking at human beings it is both negative and misleading, because it ignores all the other levels of explanation. To argue that a certain kind of behaviour is 'caused' by brain chemicals is to deal with only one part of the problem. Questions such as 'Why is the person showing that behaviour rather than any other?', 'How does the person themself understand what is happening?' and 'What are the objective circumstances in that person's life?' are equally relevant questions, which can contribute just as much, if not more, to our understanding of what is going on.

We need to look at explanations on a social level, as well as on an individual one. The interactions of a disturbed family may throw more light on a particular case and – more importantly – let us know what kinds of help may be more effective (like, say, family therapy) than a simple reductionist model which talks only about brain chemistry. The study of depression in London housewives conducted by Brown and Harris in 1978 showed that factors such as being at home with the children rather than working, or living as a one-parent family in a society geared for two-parent families, were a major contribution to depression. To understand why this is, we need to look at much wider social, economic and political issues. But, of course, the fact that reductionist arguments comfortably avoid questions like this is one reason for their popularity among the very right-wing sectors of society.

The other question that we have to ask when faced with reductionist explanations is: in what sense do they really explain, rather than simply telling us to accept things as given and do nothing about them? If we look, for instance, at the final outcomes of reductionist thought, we find totally static models of the human being underpinning them. Skinner's *Beyond Freedom and Dignity* argues that, since we are all pawns of our environments anyway, we might just as well make the best of it and go in for social manipulation on a massive scale; Dawkins's *The Selfish Gene* argues that lies, deceit and so on are inevitable simply because communication makes them possible and some genes may benefit from them – therefore we just have to accept it as unchangeable. And the only conclusion that neurological explanations of abnormal behaviour seem to come to is to drug or to incarcerate, or both, the 'abnormal' individual. These ideas have the flavour, not of explanations, but of static defences of existing practices.

It is for this reason that people get het up about reductionist thought. If it were just a matter of academic debate, nobody would care particularly much. Academics will always argue, after all. It's part of their job. But it is always the reductionist arguments which hit the headlines in the tabloids: 'Inner city riots caused by lead poisoning from exhaust fumes', and so on. By presenting issues in this way, they distract attention from wider social questions, and end up justifying existing practices at times when these are in serious need of change.

And as a mode of scientific thought, it simply isn't valid. To attempt to understand a cake in terms of its constituent parts is to miss out on the event of the cake. It is true that originally the cake was constructed from the elements of flour, fats, water, sugar and the application of heat. But once the cake has been made, it can neither be returned to those elements, nor do those elements 'explain' the cake, if by explanation we mean allow us to understand the cake any better than we do. It tells us nothing, for example, about the importance of a birthday cake, or a wedding cake, or the social symbolism of afternoon tea, or the cake as a neighbourly 'thank you' message. The cake is more than just the sum of its parts.

In the same way, society is far more than just the sum of individual human abilities. Flying, for instance, is well outside an individual's capacity unaided, yet through the coordination of science and technology it is a day-to-day reality. None of us can store the sum total of human knowledge, yet access to vast amounts of it is available in libraries. To argue that we can only understand society in terms of the ability of the individual human being is to argue that a very large amount of our everyday experience could not exist. Similarly, to argue that basic units, whether they are genes,

S–R links, or brain chemicals, entirely determine human behaviour is to ignore the vast wealth of alternative experience and capacity for adaptation which we encounter every day. We have not yet begun to explore human potential: why limit our understanding before we start?

Chapter 2

Reductionism and Behaviourism

Philosophically speaking, behaviourism has its origins in the associationism of the philosopher John Locke (1632–1704). Locke believed that the human being was born as a *tabula rasa* – that mentally, a human infant was a blank slate, with no prior knowledge or ideas. It is experience received through the senses, according to Locke, which provides the material which forms the human mind. By associating different experiences, complex chains of ideas can be developed, and new combinations can be found. Locke believed that all human thought and mental life were formed by such associations.

J. B. Watson, the founder of the psychological school of thought known as behaviourism, also saw the human being as a *tabula rasa* at birth; and like Locke he saw complexity as arising from the association of small items of experience. But for Locke, experience consisted of sensation and reflection: he was in accord with Descartes in seeing thinking as the essence of being human, reflected in Descartes's famous saying *Cogito, ergo sum* – 'I think, therefore I am'. For Watson, however, experience consisted of sensation only. It was derived from the original stimulus, external to the organism, and registered through the five external senses of sight, hearing, touch, taste and vision.

Behaviourism in its time

In its time, behaviourism was a radical theory which was embraced with evangelical zeal by its followers. In order to understand this, we have to look at the backdrop against which behaviourist ideas were being formulated. In terms of the dominant assumptions of the psychology of the time, behaviourism was perceived as a dynamic new approach, with the potential for leading to a better world by freeing its followers from the constraints of the old one. Broadly speaking, we can trace three separate strands in this backdrop, although not all of them were equally influential everywhere.

The first strand is the work of the 'introspectionist' school of psychology, against whom Watson made his particular stand. In America, the most significant figure of the introspectionist school was William James, whose *Principles of Psychology* had been published in 1890 and represented one of the first texts to present psychology as a coherent discipline, capable of explaining human behaviour. James's method consisted largely of introspection, and although some of his insights continue to have relevance for psychological research even today, his 'unscientific' methods were anathema to Watson.

James's underlying assumptions about the human mind were essentially nativist – that is, he assumed that it originated from genetic influences. His interest was in the structuring of experience, which he saw as being similar for everyone. Watson, by contrast, was an empiricist, taking the view that all human behaviour was learned, not innate. James also tended to concern himself with the more holistic aspects of human experience; whereas, as we shall see shortly, Watson was a reductionist to the core, believing that scientific knowledge could only be built up from a set of elemental building blocks.

The second strand in psychology at that time consisted of the psychoanalytic paradigm, which was beginning to dominate the mental health field. Originating with the ideas of Freud, psychoanalytic theories adopted radically different assumptions about evidence and scientific investigation from those accepted by ordinary 'science', including notions of 'psychological truth' and dream symbolism. The idea that human problems and behaviour could be addressed as manifestations of a deep underlying pathology whose origins could be traced back to infantile frustrations was one which, although popular with the medical profession, appeared to many psychologists even at the time to be woolly and speculative.

In Europe, and particularly England, a third strand of experimental psychology had emerged. Tracing its origins to the work of Wundt and Ebbinghaus, and developing further in Britain with the work of McDougall at Oxford, experimental psychology concerned itself with systematic laboratory investigations of human actions.

Since it modelled itself on the physical sciences whenever possible, it tended to focus on observation and measurement; and was therefore quite receptive to the behaviourist paradigm when it emerged.

There were differences, though, between experimental psychology and behaviourism. The underlying assumptions of experimental psychology were strongly influenced by the nativist legacy left by the earlier faculty psychology, which had dominated European thinking in the nineteenth century. Consequently, the experimental school continued to study such 'mentalistic' events as memory and perception, which were largely eschewed by the hard-line behaviourists of the time.

The new school of behaviourism, then, presented a very different picture of the human being to those already in existence. It challenged the rigid assumptions of the nativists, presenting a picture of the human being as open to new learning and capable of being moulded. It also challenged the negative images of the psychoanalysts, with their picture of the human mind as a repressed seething mass of impulses and emotions. To many, it appeared as a radical, liberating approach. Behaviourism stressed the malleability of human behaviour: if you had maladaptive habits, then the answer was to be found in your reinforcement contingencies, so by altering your reinforcement contingencies you could develop better habits. If everything you were was the result of learning, then it became possible to learn new things and become a new person.

The optimism of the behaviourist promise was particularly relevant at a time when social orders all over the world were changing. The social upheavals caused by the growth of industrial capitalism through the nineteenth century had produced much utopian-style debate about progress and the nature of the social order, as well as massive social unrest. The revolution in Russia in the early part of the twentieth century challenged feudal assumptions about power and society, and provided a dramatic impetus to social reform movements all over the world. All over the Western world, people were looking for ways to build a new society. Behaviourism's promise that people could change carried a firm implication that a new order of human society could be forged out of the old one, and it soon became firmly embedded in the new ideals of social engineering.

A famous quote from Watson's book expresses the essence of the new optimism. In 1924, he argued that if he were given *'a dozen healthy infants ... and my own specified world to bring them up in ... I'll guarantee to take any one at random and train him up to*

*become any type of specialist I might select – doctor, lawyer ... and
yes, even beggarman and thief, regardless of his talents, penchants,
tendencies, abilities, vocations, and race of his ancestors'*. The ide-
alism of this message speaks for itself. We are not limited by our
heredity: we can be anything at all, if we grow up in a world which
provides us with the appropriate learning environment.

In America, behaviourism was embraced with enthusiasm – not
by every American psychologist, but certainly by a majority. In
England, it coexisted reasonably easily with the experimental
psychology tradition, but uneasily with the deeply established
nativist school of thought originating with Francis Galton and
continuing through the work of Cyril Burt and his pupils (notably
including Hans Eysenck). In Europe, behaviourism had its influence, but never took such a hold. The reductionism of behaviourist
thinking was also, of course, directly challenged by the Gestalt
psychologists, with their emphasis on the holistic nature of experience. As a way of seeing psychology, behaviourism was generally
superseded by other theoretical frameworks, such as those offered
on one side by Piaget's genetic epistemology, and on the other by
the theoretical work of members of the existentialist school, like
Simone de Beauvoir.

When B. F. Skinner took over where Watson had left off, as the
main advocate of behaviourism, his influence was dramatic and
wide-ranging. His acceptance of the 'black box' model (stimulus
in, behaviour out) was complete. It was unnecessary to postulate
thinking at all, Skinner argued. Even language was simply verbal
behaviour – noises shaped by reinforcement, in the same way that
a pigeon's actions can be shaped through reinforcement until it
plays ping-pong. Skinner, in fact, managed to dismiss ideas of
intentionality and freedom of action completely, seeing them
simply as 'explanatory fictions' which formed convenient units of
verbal behaviour. He saw the personality as nothing but a manifestation of the individual's behaviour patterns, acquired through
stimulus–response learning. And in *Beyond Freedom and Dignity*,
he applied this model to the whole of human action in society – an
idea to which we will return.

The influence of behaviourism

At its peak, behaviourism permeated almost every aspect of psychological enquiry. Its domination probably achieved its height in

Figure 2.1   The Skinner Box, a major tool for studying S–R learning
Source: Photograph by Colin Smith.

the 1950s, although its influence had begun very much earlier. Behaviourist models challenged existing psychological theories across the board. Behaviourism is essentially a reductionist theory, and Watson's reductionism stemmed from his views on what distinguished a science. As we saw in Chapter 1, he considered that a scientific psychology should model itself on the established sciences of physics, chemistry and biology. During the previous century, each of these had been transformed by theories which had identified basic 'building blocks', and rules for how these blocks should be combined: in physics, the building blocks were atoms; in chemistry elements; and biology had been transformed into a science by the development of cell theory and Mendelian genetics. Watson saw a scientific psychology as being obliged to identify its own set of 'building blocks', and their rules of combination.

The stimulus–response (S–R) unit was the building block that Watson identified as the 'atom' of psychology. Understanding that atom, he believed, would eventually lead to a complete understanding of human behaviour. Since S–R connections had been shown to develop through learning – through Watson's own work on the Law of Exercise, and Pavlov's work on conditioned reflexes – Watson believed that learning theory would ultimately lay bare the rules of combination, showing how simple S–R units could combine into the complex actions and interactions of human life.

Following the physicists' model of the atom, or the biological model of the simple cell, Watson argued that psychology should begin by studying the simplest form of stimulus–response link. Animal learning, he argued, would be relatively uncontaminated by other kinds of factors; and so would be a suitable area of study to form the the foundation of the new science. If S–R links were the basic foundation of behaviour, then all S–R links would be similar in essence, the same way as different atoms or cells are similar in essence.

It is important to remember here that Watson's definition of the nature of science was different from the definition of science that was held by the 'introspectionist' psychologists, in that he was defining a science almost in a Popperian manner, as that which had absolute laws, basic units and rules of combination – in other words, in terms of its subject matter. The introspectionists, however, defined science in terms of the methods of investigation which were used. Psychologists such as Wilhelm Wundt, William James and Herman Ebbinghaus had established rigorous methodology and a tradition of systematic experimentation. But their subject matter – the human mind – was in Watson's eyes inherently unscientific.

At the heart of behaviourism, then, was learning theory. Skinner's work on the Law of Effect added to and augmented Watson's work on the Law of Exercise. With the introduction of Skinner's operant conditioning, everything seemed to open up for the behaviourists. When the Gestalt psychologists argued about insight learning (Köhler, 1925), behaviourists countered by talking about learning sets and generalisation (Harlow, 1949). As long as one ignored tricky issues like Tolman's work on cognitive maps or complex aspects of learning like imitation or intentionality, it seemed that the paradigm could explain every type of human learning. I have already mentioned Skinner's view of language as 'verbal behaviour' – noises were selectively reinforced from the child's earliest babbling. This, Skinner argued, applied to vocabulary too, including the social use of words like 'thought' or 'intention.' Skinner argued that, despite their popularity, these words did not reflect any underlying mental reality. Instead, they were simply manifestations of the kind of language use of which society approved and reinforced.

In the field of child development, Watson's original assertion that the child could be moulded into anything at all, given the right conditions and environment, sharply challenged both the nativist school of Arnold Gesell and the psychoanalytic orientation of Freud. The child, as we have seen, was regarded as simply a product of its stimulus–response history. Even what we would now regard as cognitive skills, such as reading and concept formation, began their psychological history with theoretical explanations in terms of stimulus–response connections.

In the mental health field, behaviourists again challenged the assumptions of psychoanalytic theory, and insisted on perceiving neurotic symptoms as evidence of faulty learning. Dollard and Miller conducted an extensive reappraisal of psychoanalytic theory, arguing that each of its tenets could be explained in terms of conditioning. As early as 1920, in one of the most ethically dubious studies in the history of psychology, Watson and Rayner had conducted their famous 'little Albert' study, and in so doing had shown how phobias could be induced. In the 1950s, Wolpe showed how conditioning principles could be applied to specific forms of disturbed behaviour, and initiated the new approach of behaviour therapy. Although the psychoanalysts made dire predictions about the recurrence or displacement of symptoms (since the underlying disturbance hadn't been dealt with at all), their patients showed quite dramatic, and apparently lasting, improvements.

Behaviourism spread its influence across the whole of psychology. Even social psychology concentrated on social behaviour, and didn't really come to grips with social perception until the cognitive revolution made it respectable in the 1970s. Studies in social psychology during the 1950s and 1960s emphasised observable aspects of social interactions, such as non-verbal communication, conformity in group behaviour, obedience to authority, and the behaviour of bystanders. It is only relatively recently that social psychologists have become so much more concerned with our understanding of social situations, such as the attributions that we make about ourselves and others, the relationships that we develop with other people, and the shared social representations which permeate social life.

Even the study of perception and memory, which almost by definition deals with the mind, adopted semi-behaviourist methodologies. Much of the research into perception during this period, for instance, concentrated on measuring aspects of sensation – looking at stimulus thresholds and reaction times and ignoring the content of what was being perceived. Similarly, despite the influence of Frederic Bartlett, memory researchers in general avoided the tricky issues posed by meaningful everyday memory, and instead looked at word-pairs and very specific – some would say trivial – recognition tasks. The theory-building which occurred in these areas restricted itself to narrow, specific areas; and it wasn't really until Ulrich Neisser published *Cognition and Reality* in 1976 that any overall attempt was made to make sense out of everyday cognitive experience.

Behaviourism's influence even extended to those who didn't share the paradigm. Many psychologists disagreed with the empiricism which was such a central feature of the behaviourist school: the nativist school was a strong one, especially in Britain, and the idea that people could change or be changed is one which goes against our traditional social assumptions (unlike in America, where it does not). So uneasy marriages developed, in which certain aspects of behaviourism were adopted while others were rejected.

In essence, behaviourism as the dominant paradigm determined what could appear on the psychological agenda. Almost all psychologists, for instance, accepted the idea that behaviour had to be objectively quantified in order to be studied scientifically; and the resulting techniques of data collection often led to sterile measures which managed to disregard personal meaning and social experience pretty well entirely. Whether or not they accepted the behaviourist paradigm, psychologists everywhere began to speak of people as 'organisms', which was an implicit acceptance of the behaviourist idea that all behaviour could be reduced to identical essential components. Behaviour was described as being 'elicited' by situations, and human beings were seen as fundamentally passive, at the mercy of environmental (or nativist) causes.

Behaviourism carried with it the idea that all human (and animal) behaviour was essentially the same; and could be treated as such. This meant that the normative group experiment came to dominate the psychological scene, discrediting the insights which could be obtained from the individual case study, or from accounts of personal experience. Ideas of replicability and reliability meant that only the more limited or predictable aspects of psychological phenomena could be discussed. This resulted in an image of the human being which entirely denied uniqueness and idiosyncrasy: something with which we are only just now beginning to come to terms. The concepts of autonomy and intentionality were rarely mentioned, except by 'heretics'; the vocabulary needed to discuss them was dismissed as 'woolly' and 'unscientific'.

Rather than opening psychology up to a new range of human potential, then, behaviourism, at least in the UK and America, ended up restricting its scope severely. It limited the methodologies of both its own researchers and those of other psychologists by defining other vocabularies as 'unscientific'. And it carried an implicit assumption about generalisability which maintained that all research had to be applied across large groups. Single-case studies, individuality and individual change were dropped from the psychological agenda, and are only just returning.

Challenges to behaviourism

While the supporters of behaviourism emphasised its promise for a brave new world, its opponents challenged it on many other grounds. One major objection made by psychologists in this country, at least, was that it defied what appeared to be common sense. Watson's insistence that anybody could be anything seemed to deny the importance of heredity, which people could see just by looking about them in physical family resemblances. It also challenged the idea of genius, and distinctive talent, which was an important social belief in a society as stratified as that of Britain.

The challenge to common sense, of course, was not one which worried the behaviourists much – perhaps rightly. After all, psychology is full of things which run counter to common sense – common sense, for instance, tells us that people will not give each other fatal electric shocks just because they've been told to by someone they don't even know! Psychological research tells us a different story. But there were more serious objections to behaviourism too.

Although behaviourism was the dominant paradigm, psychology was never unified in its support for behaviourist ideas. There were always challenges to its assumptions – many of them originating with the experimentalist school. In the 1930s, Frederick Bartlett had shown how the ability to remember meaningful information is closely linked to expectations and cultural assumptions.

This formed a starting point for a whole tradition of research which eventually led to present-day investigations of eye-witness accuracy and everyday memory. In perception, Jerome Bruner's work on expectation and the effects of personal experience showed how perception was intimately tied to the mental attributes of the individual. But these studies had to wait for the cognitive revolution to come fully into their own – and even then, they were devalued by the computer metaphor, as we will see in Chapter 9.

Opposition to behaviourism frequently took an extreme stance: Chomsky countered Skinner's assertion that infants acquire language entirely through operant conditioning with the equally extreme assertion that, on the contrary, acquiring language was almost entirely inherited and had very little to do with learning or human contact. H. J. Eysenck, although rather oddly calling himself a behaviourist, maintained that personality and even political attitudes were inherited. And even the humanistic school, while rightly emphasising a holistic view of self, ended up more or less denying the importance of environmental stimulus control in matters relating to personal growth.

Perhaps the most far-reaching effect of behaviourism in this country, though, was the way that it polarised the nature-nurture debate. Because it stated the environmentalist position in such an extreme manner, those who opposed it were given an opportunity to discredit ideas of environmental influence which they didn't fail to seize. Early psychological theory had always maintained a strongly nativist approach, and the extreme challenge of the empiricists produced an extreme reaction.

To give one example: the extreme arguments of behaviourism were – and still are – used to discredit ideas about social or environmental influence in scholastic achievement. The concept of innate 'ability' still dominates the majority of teacher training establishments and school staffrooms in Britain, and this is partly because those who opposed the idea stated their challenge in such an extreme manner. Rather than suggesting that social-environmental influences were equally important, they denied the existence of any form of individual difference in ability or talent. As a consequence, they left little room for the middle ground: a model in which talents are seen as amplified and developed by the environment. The debate became so polarised that people felt obliged to opt for one side or the other. And the dominant ideology, in Britain, was on the nativist side.

Psychology in Britain is still feeling the discrediting influence of extreme behaviourist ideas. Many sociologists, for example, still appear to believe that behaviourism is the dominant paradigm in the psychological discipline, and attack it accordingly. Many of those who undertook minor courses in psychology in the 1960s perceive psychology as a mechanistic, inappropriate discipline, because they are unaware of how much it has changed, and in particular how much it has grown away from behaviourist influences. The growth of pre-degree psychology has done, and is doing, much to inform the public about the nature of psychology; but it will be a long time before we manage to shrug off the 'either Freud or Skinner' perceptions held by so many older people.

The extreme reductionism of the early behaviourists has largely disappeared. Even modern-day 'neo-behaviourists' have, for the most part, dropped the reductionist approach adopted by Watson, and argue instead for an 'interactionist' perspective, in which cognition and environmental learning are seen to be working together to produce particular behaviours. Their emphasis is still on behaviour and S–R links, but they no longer consider that to be the only possible level of explanation in psychology.

Levels of explanation

There is a level at which many of the insights put forward by the behaviourist approach can be very useful. It is, for instance, often a good idea in changing behaviour to begin by looking at the reinforcement contingencies under which the individual is operating. The error comes in treating those reinforcement contingencies as if they were all there is. Applying the principles is one thing; accepting the inherent reductionism of behaviourism is quite another.

The behavioural level is one out of many possible levels of explanation for human experience. Human beings are complex and multi-faceted; to look for a single answer to anything is to invite trouble. We live in a culture which encourages us to look for single, 'correct' answers to things; but this is inherently misleading when we're looking at human behaviour. People don't do anything for just one single reason, even though we may often rationalise our actions that way after the event. Instead, several different levels of explanation can be operating at once.

If I want to explain a handshake, I could explain it as a conditioned behavioural response on my part to the stimulus of the other person holding out their hand when we are being introduced. But that's not the only way of explaining it. On a historical level, I could explain it as a convention with symbolic meaning: the right hand is traditionally shaken because in medieval times that allowed the two people concerned to retain their shields against possible treachery. The handshake has a socio-cultural explanation too: as a greeting and an acknowledgement of equals. If I were a neuro-physiologist, I would explain the handshake as the outcome of my brain sending a series of signals instructing bundles of muscle fibres to contract in a specific sequence. All of these are equally valid levels of explanation of the single gesture, and there are many more. To focus on one at the expense of all of the others has to be inherently misleading.

Within psychology, we use many different levels of explanation, ranging from the level of neural sensation, through habitual stimulus–response associations and cognitive levels, up to socio-cultural levels. They are all germane. An individual psychologist may choose to focus on just one level of explanation to tackle any one problem, but to insist that that particular level is the only possible or 'correct' one is arrogant and misleading. It is also dangerous, since reductionism as a style of thinking often leads to simplistic and politically questionable ideas – like, for example, the implicit totalitarianism in Skinner's *Beyond Freedom and Dignity*.

Alternatives to behaviourism

Humanistic psychologists and sociologists early recognised the questionable social assumptions underlying the behaviourist ideas, which eventually emerged most clearly in B. F. Skinner's *Beyond Freedom and Dignity*. While aiming to present a realistic attempt at discussing society, the book actually presented a picture of a world dominated by 'Brave New World'-style totalitarianism. Its basic message was that there was no room for outmoded concepts like 'freedom' or 'dignity', since none of us were really free or dignified at all. As our actions were simply the product of our reinforcement history, 'freedom' was just an illusion; so society might just as well begin to manipulate our reinforcement contingencies to produce the kind of behaviour that it wanted.

Besides raising the obvious question of 'who censors the censors' – or in this case, 'who manipulates the behaviour manipulators' – the image of the human being as a ping-pong ball, being batted around by circumstances (Bannister and Fransella, 1971), was felt by many to be simply inadequate. Psychologists began to construct alternative models: the image of the human being as an active, enquiring, theory-building scientist portrayed by personal construct theory was one; the personal growth-oriented, positively striving human being portrayed by the humanistic psychologist Carl Rogers was another.

Much empirical research illustrated the need to re-evaluate the behaviourist approach. I've already mentioned the gradual emergence of the cognitive school, which eventually led to the cognitive revolution of the 1970s and 1980s. In other fields, too, it was becoming apparent that behaviourism was not the only answer: research into behaviour therapy, for instance, showed how the relationship between the patient and the therapist was a far more significant factor in determining the outcome of treatment than the stimulus–response connections involved.

Behaviourists had always treated social influences as simply complex examples of environmental stimuli; but it gradually became apparent that social influence is in many ways qualitatively different from other types of influence. Studies of language acquisition showed how human interaction was far more important than simple exposure to language; Carl Rogers posited a need for positive regard as basic to the human being; cognitive studies showed how social factors could affect almost everything, including vigilance and attention. As evidence accumulated, it became clear that a paradigm shift was on the way.

As Thomas Kuhn informed us, paradigm shifts don't happen until there is something else to put in its place. The more the evidence accumulated for cognitive processing, the more shaky the foundations of behaviourism came to appear. Bandura and others showed how important social cognition and modelling were in human learning; and work on cognitive dissonance and attribution, as well as personal construct theory, showed how the interpretations that people put on their experience are every bit as important as the experience itself. Much of this research had taken place during the behaviourist heyday, but gradually the evidence for the new paradigm built up to critical mass.

With the advent of the cognitive revolution of the 1970s and 1980s, cognition came to replace behaviour as the focus of psychological attention. Building on the groundwork of the Gestalt school and the experimental psychologists of earlier decades, such as Tolman, Bruner, Bartlett and the like, the concept of 'mind' was firmly re-established, signalling a gradual demise of behaviourism, at least in its pure form. But we are only now beginning to re-examine our methodology and language, and in many ways, the wide-ranging legacy of behaviourism, both in vocabulary and methodology, is still very much with us.

Chapter 3

Understanding the Genome

Reductionism, as we have seen, is an approach to knowledge. It is a way of explaining things – why experiences, events or objects are as they are. But it is a very specific way of explaining things, which does so by focusing on their component parts. To be more exact, reductionist explanations *only* look at the component parts of what they are trying to explain. They are all about reducing a given thing, or phenomenon, or an experience, down to its basic elements. Once they have done that, the reductionist point of view considers that it has been fully explained.

As we saw in Chapter 1, reductionism has a long history, going back to the ancient Greeks. It takes the approach that when we understand the component parts of anything – the 'atoms' which make it up – then we will understand everything there is to know – or, at least, everything important. As a style of thinking it is very attractive, because it treats knowledge as a kind of massive jigsaw puzzle. All we need to do, reductionists believe, is to get hold of the separate pieces, fit them all together, and lo and behold! We will have a complete picture of what is going on.

The problem, though, is that things don't work like that. Yes, of course it is helpful to understand component parts. We couldn't even begin to understand the human brain, for example, if we didn't know anything about the structure of neurones and how they work. But understanding neurones doesn't tell us everything about the human brain. Different parts of the brain are made up of neurones grouped together and organised in special ways, and those different parts mediate different functions. Moreover, the ways that different parts of the brain work together sometimes form whole systems, which affect wide areas of the body or of behaviour. Understanding the neurone on its own isn't enough to let us know about those.

Emergent properties

Understanding the parts is not enough, because once we start combining different bits together, we find that there are new properties which emerge from the combination. A cake may be made up of butter, flour and sugar; but once the cake has been made, it has other properties which butter, flour and sugar don't have. A birthday cake, for example, has a special set of meanings, and those meanings are not properties of the ingredients.

We call these emergent properties, because they emerge when different elements of one sort or another have been combined; and because they are not part of those original elements. The fight-or-flight response, for example, is an emergent property of the autonomic nervous system and the different parts of the body which it reaches. It happens as the body responds to a perceived threat, by activating all of its energy-producing mechanisms at once. But it isn't contained in the neurones themselves. It is in the ways that they, and the glands, combine to work together.

Similarly, human society consists of the actions of single individuals all combined together. So understanding individual people is important, but it isn't enough to understand everything about society. We also need to recognise that there are emergent properties which come about when lots of people combine together – bureaucratic systems, for a start, and alienation, and traditions, and all sorts of other things which make society very much more complex than we could possibly realise if we only looked at individual people.

Levels of explanation

Reductionist thinking ignores emergent properties. What it does, instead, is focus on one particular set of 'elements' or components, and says that all we need to do to understand what is happening is to understand that particular set. But that ignores other levels of explanation, and, as a result, it distorts our understanding.

Levels of explanation are the ways that we go about trying to understand something. Every researcher tends to focus their work mainly on one level of explanation. But that doesn't mean that they think that their own particular level is the only one there is. The list which follows highlights a number of different levels of explanation, and there are psychological researchers exploring aspects of human behaviour at just about all of them (except perhaps quantum mechanics!) But most of those researchers are aware that their particular level of explanation doesn't tell the whole story – that it contributes to our understanding, but that there is more to say at other levels too.

Levels of explanation	
Cultural	e.g. national identity or religious conventions
Socio-political	e.g. social class or economics
Sub-cultural	e.g. social representations
Socio-cognitive	e.g. attributions
Social	e.g. conformity and obedience
Interpersonal	e.g. non-verbal communication
Personal	e.g. personality, intelligence, self-concept
Behavioural	e.g. actions and habits
Conative	e.g. plans and intentions
Cognitive	e.g. reasoning and memory
Affective	e.g. feelings and emotions
Biological	e.g. evolutionary processes in brain development
Physiological	e.g. arousal mechanisms in fear and anger
Biochemical	e.g. brain chemicals in schizophrenia
Atomic	e.g. electrical transmission in nerve cells
Quantum mechanics	e.g. sub-atomic influences

Every now and again in psychology, though, we come across people who insist that their particular level of explanation is the only one which counts. That was the case with the behaviourists, and in particular Watson and Skinner, who argued that once we understood the basic learning processes which shape behaviour, we understood all we needed to know about human beings, and nothing else was necessary. We looked at their arguments, and their weaknesses, in the last chapter. But what they did was to focus on one level of explanation – the level of habits and learned associations – and treat all the others as if they were simply artefacts – nothing more than habits and learned associations.

In reality, of course, human behaviour is much more complex than that. Our cognitions, our social understanding, our culture and many other factors influence our behaviour, and these are not simply more sophisticated variations of reinforcement contingencies. Or at least, even if they are, they have emergent properties which can't be understood simply by exploring reinforcement contingencies on their own. The behaviourist view was attractive because the mechanisms it suggested were nice and simple, and fitted with the modernist thinking of their time; but it wasn't exactly adequate.

Reductionism may hark back to an old-fashioned way of looking at the world – a way that believed that everything would come down to nice, simple elements – but it is still all around us. In this book I discuss several different sources of reductionism in psychology, including neurological reductionism related to schizophrenia, genetic determinism, and social reductionism of the sort that we find in social impact theory.

In this chapter, I want to look rather more closely at a particular source of reductionist argument which we can find both in psychological theorising and in everyday discussion. This is genetic reductionism. It comes up in several contexts, and I have written about some of these in detail elsewhere, such as the idea of inherited intelligence, for example, and the damage that particular type of reductionism has done in the past. But here we are concerned with two types of genetic reductionism in particular. The first arises from the findings of the human genome project – or rather, from simplistic reporting and interpretation of those findings. The second is the form of genetic reductionism found in what used to call itself sociobiology and has now adopted the name of evolutionary psychology.

The human genome project

Let's begin with the human genome project. This is a massive research project aimed at mapping out the whole of the human genome – that is, to identify and categorise the millions of genes involved in human heredity. A gene in this case is a segment of DNA, which is located on a specific chromosome in the nucleus of the body's cells.

Each cell of the body contains the same set of millions of genes; and between them, it is often claimed, they carry the complete pattern for the body's development. These genes are often referred to as 'units of heredity', but what each of them actually does is to stimulate the synthesis of a particular protein or enzyme in the body. It is the operation and cooperation of these proteins or enzymes which produce physical development.

The scientists working on the human genome project are well-aware of the dangers of reductionism. But the way that their work is reported in the media is often far less particular. What we increasingly hear is that scientists have found a gene 'for' something, with the implication that they have found a clear and unequivocal cause for it. We have heard about genes for breast cancer, for alcoholism, for manic depression, for musicality, and even for homosexuality. The implication, in the reports, is that these genes are the entire reason why these things happen.

The real picture, however, is much less simplistic. Basically, there are several things wrong with that reasoning. The first, and perhaps the most important, is a confusion of correlation and causality. Every psychology student learns that correlation is not the same as causality – two things may happen together, but it doesn't mean that one causes the other. For example: the manic depression gene question is the correlation between the finding that manic depression runs in families, and the finding of a particular gene which also runs in the same families and seems to produce a protein synthesis which may be involved in the production of brain chemicals involved in manic depression.

So let's look at these issues more closely. Firstly, the finding that manic depression runs in families does not automatically mean that it comes from an inherited gene. Families also bring up children, and children learn a great deal about social behaviour, emotional expression and coping mechanisms from the behaviour of those around them. So manic depressive patterns of responding will be learned by children in families with manic depressive members from quite an early age.

At the same time, the gene 'for' manic depression will be present in the body. But genes don't work all the time, automatically – their functions are switched on when the body demands it. The fact that the gene is present, though, means that when an individual is adopting a manic depressive-style response to stressful events, it will become active, and produce the relevant chemicals.

So the gene is certainly involved in the manic depressive reaction; but to say that it causes it is to go distinctly beyond the data. It is the combination of learned responses, genetic predispositions and environmental stressors which produce the manic depression. In a situation without environmental stressors, neither the learned responses nor the genetic predisposition will be activated. Similarly, there are many women with the gene 'for' breast cancer who remain perfectly healthy all their lives; and there are people with the gene 'for' alcoholism who never experience that problem, because they control their drinking carefully, abstain altogether, or simply don't see alcohol as a way of coping with problems.

It works on the positive attributes too. John Sloboda and his team of music psychologists have found that innate talent sometimes seems almost irrelevant to the development of musical excellence. What counts is the amount of practice the child puts in, and the key figure here is something like six thousand hours. Just about any child who puts in that amount of practice, Sloboda argues, will become an excellent musician. There may be a gene 'for' musicality, but without the practice time, that gene isn't going to have any effect at all.

This argument is often countered by those who point out that musical talent often runs in families, so it must be the gene which causes it. But as we have seen, families also provide environments for bringing up children. Most average children would never put in that amount of practice – about three hours a day. Children putting in that much work are going to be in families which support and encourage that sort of activity. That means they need to be in families which recognise the value of dedicated practice, and that means that those will often be families which have already produced musicians. Someone with a gene for musicality who grew up in a family which didn't have that appreciation of the importance of practice might easily be 'musical', but might only ever express that through appreciation of recorded music and never become a competent musician.

So having a gene 'for' something doesn't mean you will automatically develop it. It does give you a predisposition towards it – making you more vulnerable to it, if it is a disorder; or making you more likely to develop it if it is a positive attribute. So it affects preparedness – how ready you are to develop the thing in question. But that preparedness will be completely irrelevant unless you experience the relevant environmental situations too – stressors in the case of vulnerability to mental or some physical disorders; or facilitative environments in the case of music, art or literacy. Family influence counts, not just because families transmit genes across generations; but also because they provide environments for children to grow up in.

Evolutionary psychology

There are other aspects of genetic reductionism, too. One of them is the attempt by some people to set human behaviour in its genetic, evolutionary context. There's nothing wrong with that, as far as it goes. I used to call myself an evolutionary psychologist, and I certainly base a great deal of my understanding of human beings in an evolutionary context. But in recent years, the term evolutionary psychology has been hijacked by a school of thought which means something very different.

What this school of thought aims to do is to 'explain' human behaviour as being the product of our genetic heritage. It has a long history, dating from the work of Konrad Lorenz, and including the scientifically dubious work of the sociobiologists who claimed that human beings are 'just' the product of their selfish genes. I have discussed those specific types of genetic reductionism elsewhere in this book. But the message of the evolutionary psychologists is much the same: our genetic heritage 'determines' our behaviour, and therefore society ought to recognize that as an essential part of human nature.

Curiously enough, though (and strangely like their predecessors), evolutionary psychologists rarely describe the more positive aspects of human behaviour – people helping one another in crises, engaging in positive social interactions, and so on – as being inevitable features of human nature. Instead, they focus on all the nasty ones. Much of their work emphasises the inevitability of aggression – competition between males, competition between social groups and inter-sex aggression. I have even come across evolutionary psychologists claiming that rape is a natural consequence of the male's evolutionary drive to spread his offspring as widely as possible. But any exploration of the science underpinning these ideas shows just how pseudo-scientific they really are.

The source of the argument is the idea that (a) genes determine behaviour, and (b) genes always act to further their own interest at the expense of any other consideration. There are any number of reasons why this is complete scientific rubbish. The first of these is, as we have seen, that genes do not produce behaviour directly. They interact with the environment, so possessing a gene 'for' something doesn't say anything at all about whether it will actually produce any kind of effect. Geneticists have always known that genetic determinism of this kind is plain silly but, sadly, many psychologists have never quite caught on.

Another reason why this type of genetic reductionism is such drivel is that genes act in many different ways, in many different species. Evolutionary psychologists, like the sociobiologists before them, tend to take their examples from a very few species, who coincidentally happen to act in very sex-stereotypical ways. So they will talk about the behaviour of baboons, for example, who sometimes have a social organisation based on a very aggressive and rigid dominance system; but ignore the much more flexible and cooperative behaviour of bonobos, chimpanzees and gorillas, which are much closer to human beings. Or they take the highly territorial and sex-stereotypical robin for a model, while ignoring the shared crèche behaviour of ostriches, or the polyandrous behaviour of jaçanas.

The fact is that nature is full of biodiversity, and equally full of behavioural diversity. Instead of focusing on the behaviour of a few species, and arguing that this type of behaviour is virtually inevitable in human beings because it must be genetically advantageous, what we should be looking at is how genetic advantages can operate in the context of such a massive diversity of behaviour. Even if behaviour was genetically determined – and we'll be looking at even more of the weaknesses of that sort of argument in Chapter 13 – that would still leave us with a massive range of possibilities.

There are, of course, people working in evolutionary psychology who don't subscribe to these extreme views. And many of those who make extreme statements to the media generally back down and express them much more tentatively when they are talking to other psychologists. 'We are only talking about possibilities', they say, or 'Of course human behaviour isn't genetically determined, just influenced this way'. But it is the public pronouncements which carry the weight, and which lead to the misplaced use of genetic determinism in public policy.

If we truly want to understand how genes can affect human behaviour, what we actually need to look at is the way that they afford the possibilities for such a range and diversity of options. Of course genes provide the possibilities for aggressive action. But they also provide the possibilities for friendliness, for peacemaking, for kindness, for sympathy, and for any number of other types of human activity. Rather than focusing on the aggression, we need to understand how all of these may be possible for human beings.

Alternative evolutionary contexts

To do this, we do need to look at genetics in an evolutionary context, but at one which looks at the behaviour in relation to the environment. Fixed genetic behaviour patterns, virtually by definition, aid an animal to survive in a fixed type of environment. But if that environment changes, what is helpful for survival in one context may become a death-warrant in another.

Animals, though, are able to learn, and learning, above all else, is a way of changing behaviour. Instead of having to reproduce fixed action patterns, animals which can learn become able to change their behaviour as the environment requires – or demands. Even the most primitive animals can learn, and it is not unreasonable to say that learning is as fundamental to animal behaviour as genetics is.

But the two don't act in opposition. Rather, they act together to maximise the organism's chances of survival. In Chapter 14 we'll be looking at imprinting, and at critical and sensitive periods, which are one way that genes and learning work together. Through the sensitive or critical period, the genes shape when the learning is likely to take place, and what type of learning it is likely to be. But what is actually learned depends on the environmental situation the animal finds itself in.

Similarly, there has been a considerable amount of work on preparedness in learning. This ranges from research into one-trial learning, which shows how very readily we learn to avoid a particular foodstuff after just one unpleasant experience, to studies of preparedness in learning of honey bees, showing that they learn from scents most strongly, colours next, and shapes least readily. They are able to learn from shapes in the end, but they are much more prepared to respond to scents and colours. Preparedness in learning is another case of learning and genes working together.

Human beings are distinguished by adaptability. Human beings manage to survive in a range of climates and ecosystems, from deserts to tropical forests; from arctic tundra to temperate farmlands. If we inherited our behaviour patterns, this would simply not be possible. But we don't. What we inherit instead is a powerful tendency to learn from other people. From our very earliest days, we fixate on others, and begin to learn from them, and this learning continues throughout life. The result is an incredible adaptability, which has allowed human beings to spread out all over the globe.

There is a strong genetic component to the sociability of the human infant – as indeed there seems to be to human sociability in general. Basic emotional communications seem to be universal; language and tones of voice are used as much to convey social reassurance

FIGURE 3.1   Family resemblances can show strong genetic influences
Source: Photograph by Raymond Douse.

as to convey semantic content; and people everywhere show a readiness to band together into communities and social groups.

But what a complex social life also does is to provide a powerful environment for learning. And our genes provide us with a powerful tool for performing that learning – the human brain. Different experiences shape different skills, and the brain is tremendously open to experience. For example, Blakemore and others have shown that many of our visual nerve cells respond to the experiences they receive. About 10 per cent of cells in the visual cortex have a fixed, genetically determined function, usually related to being able to distinguish figures against backgrounds. The other cells adapt their functioning to the environment in which they are placed. So Westerners, for example, develop a disproportionate number of visual cells devoted to the detection of vertical and horizontal lines and have relatively fewer cells for lines at other angles; while people living in traditional societies develop accurate perception of lines at all sorts of angles (Annis and Frost, 1973).

Similarly, Western children are systematically trained in seeing and in sounds. They learn to name colours, to draw, to make musical sounds and so on from a very early age. Their other senses, though, generally receive much less attention. But Native Australian children are given a similar education in smell as well, and, as a result, they develop a far more sophisticated understanding of the smells around them than Western children have.

The probability is that a brain scan would show a far more developed use of the olfactory cortex in Native Australians than in Westerners, and probably – knowing the way that different nuclei in the brain develop in response to stimulation – a more developed olfactory cortex itself. That isn't because Native Australians are genetically different. It's because the brain responds to the training and experiences they have had, in the same way that muscles respond to the demands we put on them.

To talk about human behaviour as if it were genetically determined, therefore, is clearly rubbish. It is influenced by genetic factors, of course; but those factors act to give us a range of possible behaviours and a wide range of choices of action. We learn from others around us, and from our own experiences, and we shape our behaviour accordingly. To try to explain human behaviour purely in terms of the genetic level of explanation is to misunderstand in a very fundamental way what is going on.

Genetic reductionism and its implications

These examples of genetic reductionism may sound relatively innocuous. But genetic reductionism isn't a trivial affair. It has killed millions of people in the past, and continues to do so. Genetic reductionism has been the theoretical basis of the Nazi death camps, the American compulsory sterilisation laws, the murder of psychiatric patients in the Far East, and ethnic cleansing policies in the Balkans and elsewhere in the world. It underlies racist social policies and most restricted educational access systems. And it seriously distorts our social understanding of mental illness, of cancers, and of other health issues.

The fact is that causality isn't that simple. Human behaviour is always complex and multilayered, and people are as they are for a whole variety of reasons. Genes are part of the story, but they are a very long way away from being the whole of it. The human genome project offers us the possibility of broadening our understanding in a fascinating way; but we do need to bear in mind that combinations of genes are not the whole story. The emergent properties which become apparent at other levels of explanation are part of the whole, and attempts to understand genetic functioning need to be able to key in with those as well.

Reductionism as a mode of argument is popular because it makes everything seem nice and simple. But that simplicity is very danger-ous. And it's also very restrictive. We are only just beginning to understand the fascinating potential of human behaviour, so it seems to be a little pointless if we limit our understanding before we really get started.

Chapter 4

Ethical Issues in Psychological Research

Ethical issues in psychology became increasingly important in the last part of the twentieth century, and are now firmly established as a significant part of modern psychology. Not only do they feature as an area of study in their own right, but all psychological research is increasingly under scrutiny with regard to its ethical implications. Studies which were once regarded as acceptable are no longer considered to be so; and concepts like social responsibility and equity have entered the psychological vocabulary – not before time, many would say.

History and context

This state of affairs has developed for several reasons. In many ways, concern with morals and ethics has arisen throughout modern society – they are part of the current Zeitgeist. Perhaps the political exposure to monetarism and free-market economics in Britain and America stimulated such concern, by its very obvious lack of consideration of alternative values; perhaps it was a reaction to the dogmatic materialism of the middle part of the twentieth century; or perhaps it was the youth-culture 'peace and love' value-system of the 'sixties taking a more mature form. Perhaps, even, it arose in response to the increasing threat to civil liberties through tougher legislation. What is most likely is that it was a combination of all of these; but whatever the reason, the late 1980s showed a dramatic increase in media discussion and debate about ethical issues in the media. And psychology, as we have seen before, is as susceptible as any other discipline to changes in the mood of the times.

Another, related, factor was the increasing support gained during the 1970s and 1980s for the social responsibility of science movement. This movement calls into question the whole notion of 'value-free' science. It argues that science is always located within a social context, and therefore always has social implications. Perhaps oddly, it was governmental opposition to the inclusion of social responsibility of science in the school curriculum at the beginning of the 1980s that clarified much of its support among science teachers in the UK. While seeking to defend something that had only vaguely been seen as an important issue, people became very much clearer about exactly what the important underlying principles and concepts were. Given such general concerns, it was inevitable that psychology, with its explicit claims to be a science, should come under the ethical microscope as well.

The impact of the humanistic school in psychology introduced an additional emphasis on the human being who collaborated with the researcher by serving as 'subject' in psychological research. Humanistic psychologists took issue with the objectification of human beings in conventional psychological research, in which their identity as thinking, reasoning and autonomous individuals was denied. They objected to reductionist research paradigms which focused purely on some fragment of behaviour, denying entirely the social and human context of what was going on. And they emphasised that these were people, not inanimate lumps of matter. The increasing recognition that the source of psychological information was people rather than 'subjects' went hand in hand with an increased acknowledgement that these people had rights of their own, which should be respected.

Another source of ethical concern arose from psychological research itself. During the 1960s, a number of studies were undertaken which brought ethical dilemmas clearly into focus by virtue of the way in which those ethical issues had been ignored. Other psychological studies were conducted which investigated ethical questions explicitly and made known the implications of their findings. And a third set of psychological research investigated the social and other effects that well-known pieces of psychological research had produced; and brought out ethical implications arising from those. The outcome of all of these factors was a very significant shift in emphasis in psychology, away from the notion of 'value-free' science and towards the principle of ethical responsibility for psychologists.

So what implications does this have for the study of psychology? The paradigm shift which has emerged impinges on the typical psychology student in three ways: firstly, in the form of the accounts of existing psychological research which are studied as part of a typical psychology course; secondly, in the form of questions about how ethical considerations arise in practical work; and thirdly, in the form of the wider ethical issues, in society as a whole, which are raised by some of the general perspectives and themes within psychology.

Ethical questions raised by past psychological research

Introductory psychology courses, like introductory courses in other disciplines, trace how thinking has developed in the subject. They explore how generally accepted ideas and concepts have emerged, and the previous psychological research on which they are based. Typically, therefore, covering a topic at an introductory level involves looking at some of the early ideas and some of the key studies which are considered to provide the evidence on which a psychological theory was built. What this means, of necessity, is that as students study introductory psychology, they learn about psychological research which was conducted many years ago, in a very different social context.

Psychology as a discipline, however, has changed over the years. And, as psychology has changed, so has our awareness of methodology. Most students learn, for instance, about the power of the self-fulfilling prophecy and the need to avoid experimenter expectations affecting the outcome of an experiment. But the studies which demonstrated self-fulfilling prophecies so convincingly were conducted in the 1960s, which means, by definition, that studies conducted before that date did not take the possibility of experimenter effects into account. (*That's* why students are expected to know the dates of studies – it isn't just a novel form of torture inflicted on those taking exams!)

Ethical concerns, in their current form, are a relatively recent development in psychology. So many of the studies which a student learns about as part of an introductory psychology course raise ethical questions. While we can still learn from such studies – and indeed, we ought to learn from them – we have to bear in mind that it would no longer be acceptable for a psychologist to conduct such research today. While we need to see these studies as a significant part of psychological knowledge, we also need to bear in mind that modern psychology is rather different.

In essence, the difference between modern psychology and older forms of knowledge hinges around respect for the person who participates in the research – those who were traditionally called 'subjects'. The traditional forms of investigation within psychology involved a highly manipulative mind-set, in which the experimenter pulled the strings and the 'subjects' (ideally) danced. Inputs were changed and outputs measured, as if the person were little more than a lump of metal or a plant. This way of regarding research participants, as essentially passive and manipulated by the experimenter, also incorporated the idea that, as long as one didn't actually damage the people concerned, it didn't really matter what kind of thing the researcher did with them.

This lack of respect for research participants shows in a number of studies. One which illustrates it quite clearly was the well-known library study of Felipe and Sommer (1966). This study involved researchers going into libraries and deliberately invading the personal space of library users, by sitting extremely close to them, and timing how long it took before they packed up their books and moved away.

This is, of course, not a harmful thing to do – nobody was damaged, although understandably many of the subjects were irritated. But it illustrates very clearly the lack of respect for subjects in the old experimental paradigm. The library users were people carrying on with their own lives, who had a right to get on with their work in peace. But this was not considered. It was taken for granted that the experimenter had the right to disrupt other people without any consideration for their rights as individuals. If we look through the psychological literature, we find that this was a recurrent attitude, although not one which was inevitably shared by all psychologists.

Another research practice which was common in the psychological literature but which has become much less acceptable now is that of deception. Even as children, we are taught that lying to people is morally wrong and compromises one's personal integrity. But psychologists of the old school appeared to forget that, or to consider themselves 'above' it somehow. Deception was a routine aspect of psychological research, so there are many examples which I could give. But it became so accepted that it was often employed in situations where it was entirely unnecessary.

For example, take the 'bogus pipeline' technique, described in a number of textbooks (though not mine) as just another, fairly routine, way of measuring attitudes. Developed by Jones and Sigall in

1971, this technique involved first giving participants some kind of general attitude questionnaire, and then following it up several weeks later in an apparently different context. On the second occasion, participants were connected to an impressive-looking machine by means of electrodes, and told that the machine could measure tiny electrical changes associated with their 'true' attitudes. Then they were given a number of statements (actually rephrased versions of their previously expressed attitudes) as 'evidence'. This was aimed to convince them that the machine worked, so that they wouldn't bother lying.

Again, this is not a technique which is likely to cause participants deep psychological damage. But it does involve gratuitous deception, and for no particularly good reason, since there are other, far more effective ways of measuring attitudes. It reveals again the underlying attitude of disrespect, almost contempt, which the old-style psychology had for its 'subjects'.

I have chosen reasonably innocuous examples of these two principles, because it is too easy to cloud the issue by using dramatic examples. But there are many examples of research in psychology which had more potentially serious outcomes. Take, for instance, the study on self-esteem and attraction conducted by Walster, in 1965. In this, female students were given personality tests, and later asked to wait outside an office for their result. While they were waiting, they were approached by a good-looking young man – a confederate of the experimenters – who chatted with them and eventually asked them for a date. They were then given false feedback from their personality tests, designed to lower or raise their self-esteem, and asked to assess the attractiveness of a set of people, including the young man they had just met.

This study incorporates both the lack of respect for participants, and the gratuitous use of deception. But more importantly, it does it in such a way as to produce a certain amount of personal distress – experiencing a lowering of self-esteem is not pleasant – and some risk of harm, since low levels of self-esteem have been shown to have a number of psychologically damaging effects. When one examines the ethical implications of what appears on the surface to be a relatively innocuous study, and is certainly a fairly typical one for the time, the contempt which is being demonstrated for the participants is quite striking. At the time, the study passed without comment. It wouldn't be considered acceptable research at all nowadays.

There are a number of other issues which could be discussed here. For example, the anxiety caused to participants during Asch's conformity studies is often unrecognised; yet both the original papers and the Perrin and Spencer follow-ups of the 1980s record how distressed participants became during the procedure. Indeed, the question of distress was one of the first issues raised in the correspondence between Perrin and Spencer and Solomon Asch when discussing their research findings. The fact that participants had become just as distressed as those in Asch's original study at failing to conform, yet had nonetheless stuck to their individual judgements, was a significant contribution to the conclusion that Perrin and Spencer had encountered a cultural effect.

There are, of course, several even more dramatic examples of unethical practice in psychological research – Watson and Raynor's study of little Albert, for example. Admittedly, nine-month-old little Albert was deliberately selected because he was a phlegmatic kid, who had never been known to get upset over anything. But that's no excuse for deliberately subjecting the child to all sorts of unpleasant experiences designed to induce terror! According to their original paper, Watson and Rayner never actually did get the chance to recondition little Albert, as he was removed from the hospital by his mother before they had a chance. Not, however, before little Albert had become nervous, jumpy and easily upset. One wonders if his mother's trust in the integrity of the researchers had finally become eroded, after eighteen days of Albert being exposed to increasingly distressing stimuli. But this aspect of the study went largely uncommented on for many decades.

In fact, some of the studies which did generate comment sometimes seem to have been conducted much more carefully. Baumrind's criticisms of Milgram's obedience experiments, for instance, were based on possible outcomes – what might have happened, rather than what really did happen. Milgram kept in touch with all his participants, and in a survey conducted a year later, 99 per cent of them reported that they were glad to have taken part, even though it had been stressful at the time. But, of course, the essence of Baumrind's criticism was that such an outcome could not have been predicted. Even if it all worked out for the best, taking risks with people's well-being is not acceptable professional practice. It was studies like Milgram's which brought this to psychology's attention – and which, ultimately, stimulated our current concerns with ethics.

Re-evaluating research practices

But there are costs to be calculated, and Milgram's work is a good example of these. Milgram found things out about the power of obedience which were entirely unpredictable. Indeed, when professional psychologists and psychiatrists were asked to predict the likely outcome of the study before it took place, they were wildly inaccurate, as were members of the general public. Milgram's studies transformed our understanding of the social side of human nature and of the nature of power. We need, therefore, to learn from those studies, even while recognising that a modern study of obedience would require a different approach.

Similarly, not all deception is unacceptable. What about participant research, in which the researcher becomes involved in a social group as a participant, rather than as an observer? This inevitably involves some degree of deception, yet sometimes this is the only way that information about social practices can really be obtained. For instance, look at the famous 'natural experiment' by Festinger, Riecken and Schachter, in which they investigated what happened to the beliefs of a 'Judgement Day' cult when their prophecy was not fulfilled. The cult firmly believed that the world would be destroyed by flood and fire on a specific date. In readiness for this, members of the group sold their homes and possessions and gathered on a hill to await the event.

Festinger and his team posed as members of the cult and joined them on the hill. When the date came and no such cataclysm occurred, they were admirably placed to see how the group's overall faith remained consistent, but was preserved by changing the minor details, much in the manner predicted by dissonance theory. Maintaining that it was their actions which had caused the world to be saved meant that members of the cult could continue to exist without loss of face.

Participant research simply couldn't work if the researchers were to declare their intentions beforehand. So the question is whether that deception is automatically wrong. Nowadays, if a research problem requires deception, the precise details of it will need to be approved by an ethics committee, and if there is any other way, it will be sought. As a general rule, only participants who have consented to the deception can be used (an issue which I shall come back to later), and it is always required that they should be fully debriefed after the event. As participating human beings, that is, after all, their right.

In other words, making ethical decisions isn't simply a matter of applying a rigid rule. The reason why we need ethics committees is because we need to apply judgement – and for that, more than one person's point of view is needed. Even though we can't simply assume that the end justified the means, as those early psychologists did, equally, we can't entirely ignore the ends either. Reynolds (1982) argued that we should examine ethical issues in social research in the light of the three criteria in this list:

Criteria for judging ethical aspects of social research

1 **Utilitarian, cost–benefit criteria** – do we learn more from the research than we could do from research carried out differently, and if we do, is it worth it?

2 **The effects on the participants** – what will the outcome of our research be for the participants involved? Clearly, if covert observation has no effect whatsoever, this is different from research in which the covert intervention produces change.

3 **Issues of individual integrity** – have we had to engage in personal dishonesty and manipulation, and if so to what extent may this be offset by humanitarian considerations?

None of these three can be taken in isolation as the only criterion for making ethical judgements. Applying strictly utilitarian perspectives isn't acceptable – you can justify anything that way, and it was the utilitarian perspective which was the basis for much of the undesirable research in the past. At the same time, utilitarian arguments can't be entirely ignored, either. Sometimes, what we would learn is really important.

Looking purely at the effect on the participants simply isn't enough, either. There might, for example, be forms of research which we would consider to be ethically unacceptable even if the people concerned were not actually affected by it. In this context, for instance, we might still consider the Milgram studies to be unethical despite their apparent lack of damaging effects on the participants.

Reynolds discussed how these three criteria might be applied to a real piece of research by looking at Rosenhan's 1973 study 'On being sane in insane places'. In this study, a number of researchers attended various psychiatric hospitals, complaining of hearing voices. Once inside the hospitals, they dropped all such pretence, and acted as normally as their environments permitted. They were almost all diagnosed as schizophrenic, and their normal behaviour, which was not the norm for the hospital setting, was frequently taken as 'evidence' of the illness.

Taking Rosenhan's study and applying Reynolds's analysis, it is possible to argue that the information which was gathered could not be obtained in any other way, and that functionally it was valuable in alerting the professional world to important areas of doubt in psychiatric diagnosis. The whole issue of medical labelling presents a number of ethical problems in its own right, and this study highlighted some of them. It is also possible to argue that any ill-effects of the study would have accrued to the researchers alone: it was they who were diagnosed as mentally ill, and entered into a powerless relationship with the medical establishment. On the third criterion, inevitably there was untruthfulness – professions were concealed as well as the false symptom reports – but the use that was made of the knowledge was careful, individuals were not identified, and information which could be embarrassing to specific individuals was not revealed.

The work on the self-fulfilling prophecy undertaken by Rosenthal presents a similar case. Rosenthal's work began with a study in which psychology students were allocated rats to train at a maze-running task. Although the rats were matched for maze-running abilities, the students were told either that their particular rat was from a 'Maze-Bright' strain, or that it was from a 'Maze-Dull' one. And the rats lived up to the prophecies which had been made. Now in this case, there was clear deception – outright lying, in fact – and yet without it, we would not have become so sensitised to the wider research implications involved.

Rosenthal and Jacobsen's follow-up work with schoolchildren also involved some degree of deception, but there were no direct lies told to the schoolteachers. Instead, they were just allowed to overhear a conversation between the experimenters in which certain children were picked out as being 'late developers'. Although there is still a manipulative element here, most people would consider that it remains within the limits of acceptability. Moreover, what we learned from that study in terms of just how much teachers' beliefs can impact on students was extremely important.

There are other studies which show how covert research is sometimes the only option. Perhaps the most extreme example of this was Bruno Bettelheim's 1943 paper on social identity within a concentration camp – the one that was turned down by several journals on the grounds that it was 'implausible'. Bettelheim had spent two years in Dachau before managing to escape; and had thus had first-hand experience of what went on, and how people managed to maintain, or how they lost, their individual identities in the face of such monumental hardships. He himself found that he needed to cling on to his identity as a social psychologist very tightly, and during his time in the camp, he adopted rigorous mental strategies – including formal memorising techniques, obviously, as there was no opportunity for him to take notes – in studying the social processes that were taking place.

Bettelheim's research provides us with valuable insights into the social processes that were going on, between the guards and inmates as well as within the inmates themselves. In his view it was his duty to inform the psychological world of what was happening – so in this case, the conduct of covert research became ethically positive, not negative. Personally, I find it a pity that his paper isn't better known. And it certainly makes it clear how, sometimes, covert research is exactly what is needed.

Animal studies

There is a whole different set of ethical issues raised by the question of animal experimentation. Animal experimentation in psychology has had a long history, much of it originating with the behaviourists, who were mainly concerned with identifying the basic S–R 'building blocks' of behaviour. Since animals were, as they thought, uncomplicated by memory or experience, animal learning represented the simple, 'pure' form of the stimulus–response connection. As a result, the behaviourists believed they could learn about human learning from animal learning, much as a biologist might learn about the components of animal cells by studying a simple, one-celled animal like an amoeba. This would provide the key to human psychology, they believed, because they adopted the reductionist stance that all human experience could ultimately be reduced to stimulus–response associations.

The behaviourists concentrated on learning and conditioning; but there are other forms of animal experimentation which have been used in psychology. Many students beginning psychology are deeply shocked when they learn about, for instance, those perception experiments performed in the 1960s, which involved rearing kittens or apes in restricted environmental conditions in order, supposedly, to investigate aspects of the nature-nurture debate. But so much of psychology rested on animal experimentation at the time that issues of animal rights and cruelty received little consideration.

It was assumed without question by many psychologists, as well as by other biological scientists, that, since certain experiments could not be done without harming the victim, the only option was to use animals instead of people. The idea that one might take the option of not doing the study at all was one which received scant attention from the scientific establishment in general. At that time, it was considered to be self-evident that the acquisition of scientific knowledge was a goal in itself, regardless of the cost.

The anti-animal research arguments gathered in momentum through the 1970s and 1980s, partly as a manifestation of the growing debates about the social responsibility of science, and partly as more and more psychologists became unhappy with what was going on. As animal rights campaigns gained momentum, the value of vivisection was increasingly called into question. Singer (1976) pointed out that animal experiments, particularly in psychology, were often trivial, needlessly cruel, and didn't really contribute to psychological knowledge.

I do not propose to enter into the rights and wrongs of the medical research argument here. Everyone has their own opinion as to whether medical research on animals is justified. But there are certainly arguments – and champions – for both sides. For example, Gray (1985) showed how animal experimentation had led physiologists directly to a better understanding of how anxiety mechanisms in the brain operated, which meant that effective anti-anxiety drugs could be developed and used far more safely. And Blakemore's work on restricted visual environments with kittens increased understanding of astigmatism in human beings. Their argument is that, while animal experiments should be restricted and controlled to avoid needless suffering, to prevent all of them would be to throw the baby out with the bathwater.

Animal rights supporters counter that animal physiology is different to that of humans anyway, and just because we find a mechanism which looks similar, it doesn't mean that it is the same thing at all. So studies of, for instance, brain structure or functioning in experimental rats won't necessarily tell us anything at all about human beings. Ironically, perhaps, the strongest evidence from this comes from precisely one of those types of animal experiment. Fisher (1964) found that injections of the same neurotransmitter into the same part of the brain in cats and rats produced entirely different responses. However, given the interests of society as well as the champions of both sides, this argument looks set to run and run.

Whatever the rights and wrongs of the case, it did produce some very positive results for psychology. The trivial, often gratuitous, animal learning experiments which were such a feature of the 1960s and 1970s – often a course requirement for the psychology student – have now largely disappeared. Ethical guidelines on animal research are now strongly enforced, and backed up by the law. Researchers are strictly adjured not to cause animals pain or distress, and there must be a serious point to the research. And only qualified laboratory personnel are allowed to handle the animals themselves.

The problem is, though, that defining pain and distress is not necessarily easy. Looking at some of the earlier studies, some of them are beyond doubt needlessly cruel. But what about Harlow's monkeys, suffering lifelong induced neurosis through being brought up in isolation? Similarly, teaching animals to use sign language is all very well, and no doubt a terrifically fun game; but what happens to the animals at the end of the experiment? Jane Goodall once gave an account of a chimpanzee, Lucy, who was brought up with human beings and taught sign language. When she grew too large, she was put in with a colony of wild chimpanzees. When a visitor she recognised came to visit the chimpanzee colony, Lucy signed desperately 'Please help. Out'.

Again, it is a matter for personal judgement. I personally am in favour of attempts to teach animals language, because I believe that it is only when we acknowledge that animals can and do communicate with us that we will begin to respect them. But I am not in favour of bringing a chimpanzee up in an enriched, affectionate environment and then suddenly pitching it into something entirely different. As with human beings, it is a question of responsibility and respect, rather than manipulation, even though that respect may take a rather different form. If a researcher needs to justify both the purposes of their research and the long-term consequences for the animals to an ethics committee, then these issues come on to the agenda. Without such requirements, they are too easily overlooked.

Student practical work

So what does this change in emphasis imply about the conduct of a student's own practical work? The typical introductory psychology course requires students to undertake a number of practical exercises which take the form of research projects. Introductory syllabuses advise that ethical considerations must be addressed in the conduct of these studies, and generally recommend that the ethical guidelines of either the British Psychological Society or the Association for the Teaching of Psychology should be followed. So let's look at some of the practical implications which are involved in taking ethical issues seriously.

Firstly, and above all else, there is the question of respect for one's research participants. That encompasses several things. For one, it involves respecting confidentiality – it shouldn't be possible to identify any of the participants from the report. In group studies, of course, participants would be unlikely to be identifiable; but more in-depth case studies can often end up dealing with quite personal issues, and it is essential that confidentiality is respected in these instances.

But respecting research participants also means making sure that the study doesn't involve anything which the research participants might find intrusive, offensive or insulting, if they knew the whole of what was going on. I have already shown how the Felipe and Sommer study was offensive in its lack of respect for research participants. The question a student needs to ask when designing a study is: are the research participants being manipulated into doing what the researcher wants, or are they and the researcher cooperating in a joint venture? And since one's own view is, by definition, biased, it is essential that other people's views are consulted in the planning stage, through an ethics committee, or the submission of an outline for approval.

Then there's the question of deception. Deceiving subjects is unethical, but what do researchers do if they don't deceive? Effectively, there are three alternatives to using deception in psychological research:

1   Tell the truth (and carry out studies which will allow you to do so without any likelihood of contamination. People are often much less motivated to lie than one might imagine from the psychological literature).

2   Reorganise the research technique so that there is no need for deception, by using different methods, like interviews, questionnaires and case studies.

3   Get your participants to grant you permission to deceive them.

On the whole the first two are easier, although Gamson, Fireman and Rytina (1982), in their study of obedience and rebellion, produced an inventive technique for getting permission from their research participants. In their study, people who had volunteered to participate in the research were contacted by telephone and asked if they would be prepared to participate in the following types of research:

(a)   Research on brand recognition of commercial products;
(b)   Research on product safety;
(c)   Research in which you will be misled about the purpose until afterwards;
(d)   Research involving group standards.

Only those who agreed to option (c) were selected for the research, although in practice that was virtually everyone. Such practices, though, are more difficult for a psychology student to achieve than they are for a professional researcher, so on the whole the first two strategies are much more appropriate.

Which brings us to the question of research techniques. Taking ethical issues seriously means moving away from the old manipulative mind-set, and into something which recognises the participants as human beings. But the traditional psychological research methods with which most people are familiar are based on different assumptions: that you can't trust your subjects, and that they need to be tricked into revealing things. We will be looking at this more closely in the next chapter.

Nowadays, though, we see this level of manipulation as largely unnecessary. More direct ways of finding things out are becoming increasingly common in psychological research. They, in turn, carry their own implications about research skills. It is remarkably difficult, for instance, to design a good questionnaire, but it's a skill which is worth learning. Introductory methods courses often include case studies, observations, interviews and questionnaires as well as experimental methods, so there is plenty of scope for adopting different techniques.

The new paradigm has also led to the emergence of alternative methodologies, like the ethogenic approach outlined by Rom Harré. Such methodologies include a greatly increased emphasis on qualitative analysis. Looking at what people say, and how they perceive and construe events, is increasingly recognised as a valid part of psychology. To look at them, we need qualitative rather than quantitative techniques. As yet, though, relatively few textbooks instruct students in how to undertake qualitative analysis, although they often go into considerable detail about how to trick and-or manipulate subjects. But this is changing.

General perspectives and themes

Then there are the wider ethical issues that are raised as psychological theory impinges on society as a whole. There isn't the scope here to go into these in detail, and we will be looking at some of them again in the next chapter, so for now I shall just make a couple of points.

The first concerns the social responsibility of science. A number of psychological theories have had very powerful social effects – which haven't always been to the good of humankind. Stephen Jay Gould's book *The Mismeasure of Man* shows how IQ theory was used from the outset as an instrument of racial discrimination; and in England, the belief in inherited intelligence propagated by Galton and Burt is still a powerful factor in the education system – acting as much through self-fulfilling prophecies as anything else. Kallman's twin studies of schizophrenia provided a direct rationale for the extermination of vast numbers of people in the Nazi gas ovens. We will be looking at all of these issues again in Chapter 12, but they show just how powerful the social implications of psychological theories can be.

Similar arguments can be made about the socio-political implications of physiological and sociobiological reductionism, and these will become apparent elsewhere in this book. The principle of social responsibility in science applies as much to psychology as to any other discipline, and the general socio-political implications of our theorising is something which all psychologists need to consider much more closely than they have done in the past.

The other side of the coin is what is left out of psychology. As a discipline, psychology has tended to be remarkably ethnocentric, focusing mainly on the psychological processes of the white North

American undergraduate. But the pluralism of modern society means that this, too, is no longer acceptable. In a modern world, respect for other cultures is an essential ethical principle. The demands of cultural awareness and multiculturalism mean that psychology needs to reflect a wider variety of cultural values, and to incorporate such values into its everyday practices: sampling, selection of research topics, the identification of problems, and so on. While this, of course, generally goes under the heading of equal opportunities, it is an ethical issue in its own right, involving as it does the implicit devaluing or ignoring of the validity of people's lives. So it too is one of the broader implications raised by psychology's increased ethical awareness.

Of necessity, this has been only an overview of some of the issues raised by ethical considerations in psychology. There are many other topics, and many other questions which can be raised. It can be argued, too, that a full acceptance of the ethical implications of psychological research actually involves a revolution in psychology, and this is the issue that we will look at in the next chapter.

Chapter 5

Changing Values in Psychological Knowledge

We have seen in earlier chapters how the nature of knowledge in the psychological discipline has changed considerably over the past 100 years, and always in line with its social context. Schools of thought, methodologies and research techniques reflect their social origins. For example, the 'armchair science' of the first, introspectionist psychologists (for example, James, 1890) reflects the tradition of the Victorian gentleman-researcher, for whom science was an intellectual pursuit and hobby rather than a profession.

Later, as the social order changed and the concept of meritocracy came to replace ascriptive values in social organisation (at least in theory) the materialist socio-political philosophies of the early part of the twentieth century were reflected in the mechanistic, 'objective' methodology of the behaviourist era, as exemplified by Watson (1913). The prevailing social belief in the ability of society to produce a brand-new and better social structure without reference to the past resulted in an empirical methodology which decontextualised human action, treating each separate behavioural incident as a self-contained unit in itself, linked to other units purely by associative chains.

In the second half of the twentieth century, the growth of the expert culture through technology, computers and professional specialism was reflected in the development of technological methodologies based on computational metaphors, with increasing complexity of experimental design and statistics, and ever more sophisticated attention to the finer details of information processing (see Baddeley (1983) as an example, although there are many other possibilities).

Nowadays, however, society is changing yet again. Just as the transition from the mechanistic concepts of progress of the first half of the twentieth century gave way to the expert culture of the second half, so the expert culture is itself giving way to a new emphasis on social responsibility. Expertise in itself is no longer enough: it is how we use that expertise which matters. Accountability is all-important. The consumer society has brought with it a new emphasis on individual choice and personal autonomy, while at the same time our growing social acceptance of cultural pluralism has brought with it the demand that those from differing cultures or persuasions should be respected.

As society comes to terms with the increasing demands of cultural pluralism and consumer capitalism, a new awareness of ethical responsibilities has come to psychology. As part of this awareness, all psychologists who are members of the British Psychological Society (BPS) receive a copy of the Code of Conduct for psychologists, which outlines procedures for conducting research and professional practice. A look at the BPS guidelines for conducting research with human beings illustrates the type of explicit ethical requirements to which psychologists are currently adapting. The guidelines are summarised here:

BPS criteria for ethical research

1 Investigators must always consider ethical implications and psychological consequences for research participants.
2 Investigators should inform participants of the objectives of the research and gain their informed consent.
3 Withholding information or misleading participants is unacceptable. Intentional deception should be avoided.
4 Participants must be fully debriefed, so that they can complete their understanding of the nature of the research.
5 Investigators must emphasise the participant's right to withdraw from the experiment at any time.
6 All data obtained must be treated as confidential unless otherwise agreed in advance.
7 Investigator must protect participants from physical and mental harm during or arising from investigations.
8 Studies based on observation must respect the privacy and psychological well-being of the people studied.
9 Investigators must exercise care in giving advice on psychological problems.
10 Investigators share responsibility for ethical treatment, and should encourage others to rethink their ideas if necessary.

Source: Adapted from British Psychological Society, 1990.

On the surface, it would seem that the guidelines simply reflect an adjustment to existing investigative techniques. Psychologists must now go about their research in different ways. But if we look at the fundamental assumptions which underlie them, we can see that the new approach is much more than that. In essence, it argues that people are not merely the 'raw material' of psychological research, to be manipulated at the whim of the scientist–psychologist. Instead, the new approach sees people as autonomous beings, able and entitled to make informed choices about their mode of action and to receive full information about their experiences (British Psychological Society, 1990).

This view of the human beings who form the subject matter of psychological research represents a radical change for psychology. Conventional psychological methodology is thrown into disorder when faced with the active, enquiring individual as its subject matter. The result is that the modern psychology student must reconcile what seem to be (and are) several inherently contradictory demands.

The nature of introductory psychology courses

The source of the confusion lies far deeper than just problems with data collection. Introductory courses in psychology, whether they be A level psychology courses or first-year 'Introduction to psychology' university courses, are the primary agents of socialisation into the discipline. It is in these courses that students learn what psychology is all about, what issues are of concern to psychologists, and how psychologists go about their work. As the student's first contact with the discipline, their primary purpose is to familiarise the student with its key ideas and assumptions.

In doing so, of necessity, these courses present a conceptual history of the subject – as do introductory courses in all scientific disciplines. They describe how key ideas and concepts have developed, the empirical basis on which they rest, those areas of knowledge which have become established within the discipline, and how enquiry into different fields has changed over time. As part of this process, they inevitably encapsulate the attitudes and methodologies of previous eras. This is true of all the sciences, not just psychology, but it is with psychology that we are concerned here. And in psychology, many of the attitudes and assumptions manifest in the history of the discipline are directly contradictory to the ideas and assumptions inherent in a full acceptance of ethical issues.

The challenge for the discipline, therefore, is how to introduce students to psychology, including its history, while simultaneously socialising them into a new ethical attitude. Meeting this challenge, I contend, involves three separate and distinct tasks. The first of these is one with which most psychologists and psychology students are familiar, and is reflected in the BPS guidelines mentioned previously: the adaptation of research techniques so that students can learn how to conduct research in an ethical manner.

Adapting research techniques

Current research psychology, at least as taught to undergraduates, operates within an empirical paradigm which is modelled on the physical sciences. The scientist manipulates her subject matter, while the subject matter remains inert, responding only to the physical changes by which it is is manipulated. A look at the basic principles of experimental research into which psychology students are inducted shows the power of this model.

One of the first things students learn, for example, is that there is a need for the researcher to maintain rigorous control over the physical situation, in order to ensure that there is 'no difference' between two experimental situations except the one being manipulated. Practical manuals and methods courses emphasise the susceptibility of the human being to unconscious social influence, and teach students about the desirability of 'double-blind' controls to prevent such influences. Tasks are decontextualised in order to ensure that the individual's previous experience or prior knowledge doesn't 'contaminate' the study. What all this adds up to is the idea that the research participant must be kept as inert as possible, responding only to the manipulations of the researcher.

The adaptation of research techniques in order to conform to more ethical standards is a process which is already taking place, and is reflected in such documents as the BPS ethical guidelines. As we can see, these guidelines challenge such well-established practices as the use of deception, the assumption that the psychologist is entirely free to determine the experience of the research participant once they have committed themselves to the research, and the idea that the expert should have exclusive access to relevant information.

However, while they are of course necessary, such adjustments to technique are not enough to ensure ethically responsible practices, since existing research techniques are predicated on the assumption that people's behaviour is inherently unreliable (in the statistical sense) and must therefore be rigidly controlled. Teaching students that the double-blind control is necessary to prevent 'contamination' of the experimental outcome directly contradicts teaching students that people are entitled to full information about what is being done to them.

Moreover, the language of traditional methodology contains powerful emotive loadings. We speak of 'contaminating' variables, of a 'well-controlled' experiment, and of 'pure' stimulus input. These phrases transmit, quite explicitly, an attitude that controlled data are inherently 'good', and that uncontrolled information is inherently 'bad'. As psychologists, we are aware of the effectiveness of vocabulary in influencing attitude, and students are introduced to these terms, and their underlying value-loadings, at a very early stage in their psychological development. The result is a deep-rooted mistrust of 'uncontrolled' information.

I would argue, however, that such control is incompatible with a true respect for the research participant. Human beings are active and enquiring, and make their own sense of what is going on. Moreover, they adapt their behaviour to the situations that they are in, including the tightly controlled situation of the psychological experiment. Irwin Silverman's book *The Human Subject in the Psychological Laboratory* shows how unrealistic it is to see people as passive, inert experimental material. But it is more than just unrealistic: it shows a deep-rooted contempt for the individual as a human being. Information which is obtained using methods which truly respect the individual as an autonomous, personal agent is by its very nature uncontrollable.

A new methodology

The implication of this is that a full acceptance of ethical issues in psychology requires a new approach to methodology. In the real world, human beings are inherently unreliable. Mood and health fluctuate, experience leaves its mark, none of us remain exactly the same from day to day. Unreliability, in the statistical sense, is a distinctive feature of the psychologist's subject matter. It is not, as it is assumed to be in the physical sciences, a function of some external or artificial 'contamination'. Real people grow, develop and change.

In our teaching, we inform students that reliability and validity are equally important criteria for psychological measurement.

In practice, however, we emphasise reliability above all else. This comes about as a direct result of our idealised view of the physical sciences. A psychological measure which is unreliable is almost automatically regarded as invalid. Yet if our subject matter is inherently unreliable, the converse is the case. And that means that to elevate reliability to the paramount research goal is to distort the realism – and the validity – of our picture of human behaviour.

These distortions have been repeatedly demonstrated, for example, by researchers such as Orne (1962) and Silverman (1977), who have shown how ignoring the active agency of human beings in the research process gives a delusion of validity which is completely erroneous. Taking ethical issues fully on board involves respecting the human being as a person in their own right, not denying their active involvement in what is happening to them by treating them as passive material objects.

I am not advocating, though, that we should abandon the quest for scientific rigour in psychological research. Rigour is essential to any scientific endeavour, and the careful collection of data is the paramount responsibility of the scientist. But there is more than one type of scientific rigour, and more than one way of collecting scientifically valid information. We need to broaden our concept of science, and recognise that there is more to scientific rigour than just controlled experimentation.

The ethical demand of respect for the human being requires a paradigm shift; and that shift is well on the way in psychology. It can be detected from a number of indices. Harré's ethogenic approach suggests taking the episode as the basic unit of social analysis, as more valid for the understanding of human experience than the single act or action. The growing acceptance of action research is another sign, as is the increased use of qualitative data to augment research of all kinds, even technologically-based psychophysiological research. As psychologists are becoming increasingly aware of the limitations of the single-cause approach to experimental design, action research, ethogenics, discourse analysis and qualitative approaches are all gaining in currency within the discipline.

Increasingly, psychological research projects combine traditional methods with qualitative techniques. Each of these has its strengths and weaknesses. Where traditional psychological methodology sacrificed validity in the quest for reliability, the new methodology, in a sense, does the opposite, emphasising validity at the expense of reliability. Both have something to contribute to our understanding of the human being, and we need a balance between the two.

The problem, however, is that introductory research method courses in psychology are only just beginning to reflect that balance; and some of them are still a long way from it. There are reasons for this. One of them is our deep-set anxiety lest we be thought to be not 'properly' scientific. Another is a lack of knowledge of how to go about systematic research in this new way. There are several different methods for conducting qualitative research, for example, yet it is only very recently that they have begun to appear in introductory methods textbooks. Students are taught first about traditional methods (emotive terminology and all) and only later introduced to qualitative techniques or 'real-world' data collection. If nothing else, primacy effects would ensure an imbalanced perception of the two.

If we are to take our ethical principles seriously, then, methods of collecting data which show respect for the experiences, ideas and background of the research participant need to be taught with at least equal emphasis with more traditional approaches. But this on its own would not resolve the problems of the psychology student struggling to reconcile ethical responsibility with psychological knowledge. There is yet another problem, and this has to do with the relationship between the discipline and its history.

Social responsibility of science

I contend that a full realisation of ethical issues also requires a higher-order appraisal of psychological knowledge and research, to locate it within its social and epistemological context. This is all to do with the social responsibility of science. As students are introduced to psychology, they are also gaining impressions of what psychology is all about. If we judge from its history, psychology is at least partly about manipulation and ethically questionable research practices.

But more than that: psychology's theories, too, have often had dramatic social consequences. For example, early theories of infant attachment, long-since modified by research psychologists, sparked off debates about working mothers which still continue today. In their time, they have influenced court judgments, family life and social policy regarding single-parent families (Rutter, 1981). Early theories about intelligence legitimated eugenic policies both in Europe and America, were indirectly responsible for the deaths of many deemed to belong to 'inferior' races in the Nazi concentration camps, and are still perpetuated in some societies today (Gould, 1981). Psychological theories of aggression and crowd psychology underlie not only the political assumptions underpinning the horrifying violence of events like Tiananmen Square, but also the policing policies which led to tragedies such as Hillsborough (Banyard, 1989).

Psychology has traditionally blinkered itself to the social implications of its theories. Many of these outcomes originate with theories which are no longer current in the discipline, so we like to think that they no longer have any relevance for psychology. Yet they are part of our history, and as much a manifestation of the social responsibility of science as is the utilisation of the atomic bomb to physics. Psychologists developed these theories, and as psychologists we have no right to walk away from their consequences – particularly not in introductory courses.

Treating psychological knowledge as if it were context-free and consequence-free is another manifestation of psychology's lack of respect for the people who form its subject matter. A full acceptance of the respect for the human being encapsulated in the idea of ethical responsibility also involves accepting the social responsibilities of psychology, not trying to pretend that psychological knowledge is in some sense independent of the society in which it occurs.

In this sense, then, if we are to realise our ethical responsibilities fully we need to recognise and learn from our history, rather than leaving it as a conceptual trap for our students. That means, primarily, that we have to identify it – both methodologically and in terms of its social implications and context. We need to stop pretending that psychological knowledge is somehow context-free and timeless. We cannot articulate the new approach without drawing contrasts with the old, and those contrasts need to be drawn explicitly. I am not arguing that psychology is in any sense a prisoner of its history, but I am arguing that we can best move forward if we acknowledge, fully, what it is that we are trying to change – that to change the present, we must first acknowledge the past.

A full realisation of ethical issues, then, involves much more than simply tinkering about with our existing research techniques. It means that the new generation of psychologists need to be socialised into a psychology which respects the human being. That doesn't mean that we reject everything which we already know. It just means that we need to acknowledge the nature, history and pluralism of our discipline. Respect for the human being as an active, autonomous individual involves a major rethinking of our approach to methodology, and a far fuller appraisal of psychology's past and present role in society than is often appreciated. Teaching students about ethical criteria for conducting research is important, but it is far from being enough.

Chapter 6

Perspectives in Social Psychology

Social psychology, during the past twenty years, has been going through a revolution. It is a quiet revolution, but a revolution nonetheless. There is a paradigm shift going on. That paradigm shift concerns the nature of social psychology, and it deals with major issues such as the question of reductionism, the value of laboratory experimentation, and how far social psychology can be considered to be truly social enough to explain human behaviour in a real society.

Traditional research

A great deal of the psychology which people study on typical social psychology courses is of the older kind – it has come from the pre-revolutionary paradigm. Someone who has done a conventional social psychology course is likely to have come across topics such as impression formation, attraction, non-verbal communication, attribution, bystander intervention and obedience. All interesting areas, and all topics which help us to understand social life. Or at least, that's how they seem on the surface.

Impression formation

But do they really? Let's look at them more closely. The topic of impression formation includes aspects of social thinking such as stereotyping and primacy effects. And nobody would dispute that these happen: we do sometimes stereotype people, and we do react to people on the basis of the first impression that we have of them. But once we've acknowledged that, what else is there to say? Not a lot. To get any further in understanding social living, we need to look into these issues more deeply. Yes, sometimes we stereotype. But equally, sometimes we don't. And sometimes, as we become aware that we are stereotyping, we make an effort to change our thinking – to stop ourselves from letting accepted stereotypes affect our judgement. We realize that people are not all the same, even if they do fit into the same category.

So what we really need to look at in this area isn't whether people are aware of large-scale social stereotypes or not – which is largely what the research described on introductory courses is all about – but when people stereotype and when they don't, how stereotypes change, why some people stereotype more than others, what purposes stereotypes serve, and how individual people change the nature of their stereotypes during the course of their lives. Not much of the social psychology on conventional courses has been concerned with this.

The same goes for primacy effects. Yes, of course we can be affected by our first impressions; and in a situation like a job interview, that can be absolutely crucial. But life doesn't really consist of nothing but job interviews, even though it may feel like that sometimes. What about the rest of the time? Some of my closest friendships have been with people whom I didn't particularly like when I first met them. I didn't dislike them, or at least not enough to avoid them, but I didn't particularly like them either. But over time, as we moved in the same circles, I got to know them better, and we eventually became friends.

First impressions, in other words, are not the whole story. We often rethink our first impressions. Sometimes we admit we are wrong, but more often, we completely forget that we didn't like the person at first – human beings have an impressive capacity for re-writing history! So my point is this: that what is really interesting about primacy effects isn't just the immediate phenomenon, as studied by those social psychologists. It's what happens over time: when first impressions stay with us and when they don't; how they influence us, and how we change them.

Attraction
The same argument can be applied to the psychology of attraction. If you look at the research which goes under that heading in an introductory psychology course, what it is really all about is the dating behaviour of the lesser-spotted North American Undergraduate. But think, for a minute, of the people that you personally like to be with – the people that you yourself find attractive. Do these studies really explain how you came to like them?

Most types of attraction in everyday living are much longer-term processes, based on a deeper social knowledge and much more social interaction. It is highly questionable whether asking people to rate photographs for attractiveness can get anywhere near the reality of social attraction.

Both of these topics, then, have suffered from being treated as if they were immediate phenomena, whereas really they are longer-term developments. The research which a student following a standard social psychology course learns about consists of superficial snapshots of social processes. But in real life, these social processes occur over time, and in a social context. Moreover, the time-span and social context are so important, that the snapshot actually bears very little resemblance to the real thing.

Another set of topics in 'traditional' social psychology concerns the processes which underlie social behaviour. Both attribution and non-verbal communication are social processes which we can see in action all around us. They are to do with how we interact with other people, and how we make sense out of what is around us. But both of these suffer from being taken out of their social context. They are treated as if they were phenomena which occur in isolation, regardless of what they actually mean in the life of the person who is engaging in them.

Attribution

Take attribution, for example. One of the approaches to attribution which a social psychology student learns about is Kelley's covariance theory – the idea that the type of cause which we identify for a particular event derives from the three features of consistency, consensus and distinctiveness. In other words, according to this model, the human being acts as a computer: we process the different bits of information, do the calculation, and come out with the result.

But in real life, attribution doesn't work anything like that. As Lalljee (1981) pointed out, explanations are always given for a reason – and that reason is directly tied to the social context. Consistency doesn't always mean the same thing. You wouldn't accept 'he always does it' as an adequate explanation for why someone had just stolen a car, would you? That just invites the question 'why?' – why does he always do it? Simply looking at distinctiveness, consensus and consistency is not enough for us to explain that event.

The same holds true for less dramatic social events too: you might accept 'she always does it' as a sufficient reason for why someone was out walking their dog at six o'clock in the evening, but that wouldn't be an adequate explanation for why she was doing it at three o'clock in the morning. The point is that we don't come to each attribution completely fresh, and simply process that information out of context. We set what is happening in a framework drawn from what we know about social life: we draw on our pre-existing social knowledge to explain what is going on. Consistency, distinctiveness and consensus may be all right for explaining why John laughs at the comedian, but they are distinctly limited when it comes to explaining why someone steals a car.

Non-verbal communication

Non-verbal communication doesn't take place in a social vacuum, either. It isn't just a matter of knowing the rules of how to interact 'appropriately', even though learning something about some basic rules can be a distinct help to those who are socially unskilled. For most people, non-verbal communication is all about meaning. It is a way of demonstrating unspoken social relationships: it signals power, control, friendship, attachment, social distancing, and a host of other messages. Taken out of that social context, the study of non-verbal communication becomes just a bewildering collection of descriptions of different signals. On their own, they have little or no intrinsic meaning. It is only when they are looked at in their social context that they mean anything.

What these examples show us, then, is that social processes cannot be studied in isolation if they are really to tell us something meaningful about how we go about living our social lives. Instead, we need to look at what they are telling us about living, and how that knowledge fits in the wider social context of the world that we live in. The type of traditional social psychology which takes these phenomena out of their social contexts doesn't really tell us very much at all.

Traditional theories

Then there are the theories. We need to look, very carefully, at the kinds of theories which emerge from social psychological research. And that highlights another major problem, which is that traditional social psychology is pretty short on general theories. It is, as

Kuhn might have said, pre-paradigmatic – what theories it does have are limited to a very narrow range of phenomena. There are not many general theories which can link together several different aspects of social behaviour. This makes it very difficult to look to traditional social psychology and gain any general sense of the person as a coherent social being. Instead, we get disparate items of information: a collection of 'ooh look ain't it interesting' bits.

Deindividuation

Take Zimbardo's theory of deindividuation, for instance. This has a relatively narrow range, being a theory which was formulated entirely in order to explain how people act in crowds. Like attraction, some of the phenomena which it is trying to explain may also be peculiarly American. To take one example: for the most part, suicides in European countries tend to do so in private, rather than by standing publicly on high buildings. And the behaviour of crowds in shouting 'Jump, jump!' at the would-be suicide may also be distinctively American. I have only heard of one instance of it happening in the UK, and that was in a very popular tourist town during the main season. Nobody, to my knowledge, checked whether the town contained a significant number of American tourists on that day.

But Zimbardo proposed deindividuation as an attempt to explain this, and also other kinds of crowd behaviour, most notably riots and the behaviour of football crowds. It is when we look at these contexts that the most significant weakness of this theory becomes apparent. Like social impact theory, deindividuation is inherently reductionist: it attempts to explain crowd behaviour purely in terms of what happens to individuals. As such, it entirely ignores other levels of explanation. The violence of political riots is seen as occurring simply because the individuals have become anonymous – and the underlying perceptions of social injustice which are an inevitable factor in such riots are entirely disregarded.

In political terms, of course, Zimbardo's deindividuation theory can be seen as a straight-line modern equivalent of Le Bon's 'mob psychology', and it can be seen as serving the same socio-political purpose. It distracts people away from asking embarrassing social questions about power, injustice and poverty, and encourages them to blame individual psychology for why the disturbance happened. So there is a socio-political dimension to this question, as well as a scientific one.

Social impact theory

One of the few attempts to develop a more general theory of social interaction is Latané's social impact theory. Latané (1981) explained audience effects, bystander intervention and the like by creating a metaphor of other people as a set of light bulbs, shining on the actor. The more light bulbs, the greater the strength of the social impact; the more influential the person, the stronger the bulb wattage; and the closer or more immediate the person, the more powerful their effect. What this theory does, in effect, is to see social influences as the sum of the influence of individuals: we can explain how people are influenced essentially by adding up who is influencing them.

But although this theory does try to link together different bits of social psychology, it does so by ignoring completely other social processes which may be influencing what is going on. While it may be true that part of the explanation for why people do or don't act to help others may simply be a result of the presence of other people, it is equally true that other levels of explanation are important factors as well. We need to look at wider social realities if we are to make sense out of social behaviour.

One type of wider social reality concerns shared social beliefs. To take just one example: the Hollywood 'but what if...?' myth of the human being as someone who 'might' do almost anything is a powerful shared belief which influences human behaviour. People are frightened to step into emotionally intense situations because they are worried that they may get into something that they can't handle, and which they might not be able to escape from. Hollywood has built up a whole industry around telling people that the most ordinary situations may land you in terrifying situations that you can't get out of. Western society is flooded with films and TV dramas based on this idea.

So it isn't altogether surprising that many people hesitate before stepping in to help a stranger. The 'what if ...' scenario has become an important factor in people's understanding of social action, unrealistic though it may be. The fact that psychological research shows how most people will actually help in a real-life situation shows that this is not the only factor, of course, and tells us something important about the basic helpfulness of people; but the study of social beliefs can also help us to to understand the people who don't help. Neither of those, though, are the sort of issue which you could deal with using social impact theory.

Levels of explanation

The big problem, then, with these traditional social theories is that they fail to link with other levels of explanation. In this, of course, they are following a long-established psychological tradition. Psychology has frequently been criticised by sociologists as reductionist, and if we look at it historically, that is true. For example, in 1920, Freud reformulated his theory of personality to include the new idea that the human psyche also contained a negative and destructive source of energies, known as thanatos, in addition to the positive life-enhancing energies of the libido, which he had described many years earlier. Freud thought it necessary to introduce this concept in order to explain the massive carnage of the First World War, in which virtually a whole generation of young men was wiped out.

Social and political theorists, however, saw no need to invoke explanations for the slaughter in terms of destructive psychological energies. They could find adequate explanation in terms of the social, political and economic conditions which were the antecedents of the war. These created a situation in which several years under the restrictions of a war economy became perceived as a workable solution to overwhelming economic problems.

That doesn't mean, of course, that psychological factors were totally unimportant. The enormous scale of the war casualties, for example, had everything to do with the retention of old-fashioned beliefs by the military command which did not keep pace with advances in technology. Sending whole battalions of troops 'over the top' in direct frontal open assaults was a tactic left over from the days of cavalry and sabre-fighting, but totally failed to take account of the development of the machine gun. It was this tactic which accounted for the millions of deaths in the First World War, in Flanders and elsewhere. Those of you who contribute to the Poppy Day appeal might reflect on the irony of its being named after the very General Haig whose outdated ideas were directly responsible for the massive slaughter and mutilation which made the fund necessary in the first place.

So I am not saying that psychology is irrelevant in these matters. What I am saying is that the type of psychological explanation which we develop must be one which can link with other levels of explanation too. It was a combination of psychological, social and economic factors which produced the carnage of the First World War, in the same way that it was the combination of psychological beliefs and social conformity with economic and sociological factors which produced the atrocities of the Second World War. The reductionist explanation leaves no room for social and economic dimensions, but they are important too.

Milgram's agency theory

To explore this idea, let's take another well-known social psychological theory – Milgram's agency theory, which he developed in order to explain his experimental findings: that people would be prepared to 'kill' another human being simply by doing what they were told. In Milgram's book *Obedience to Authority*, we read Milgram's proposal that this ability has an evolutionary origin, deriving from a need for social animals to act as members of a hierarchy. This means, according to Milgram, that each individual has two entirely different modes, or states, of operation: an autonomous state in which they act independently and in line with their own conscience; and an agentic state, in which they suppress the actions of conscience and act simply as the agents of someone higher in the hierarchy.

There are lots of things wrong with this theory, not least of which is its assumption that animal social behaviour is inherently hierarchical. Although this was a popular assumption at the time that he developed the theory, subsequent animal research has shown that, in fact, dominance hierarchies are very much rarer than was assumed in the 1960s and 1970s (Appleby, 1985), and are an unusual form of social organisation rather than an inevitable one. But Milgram was working from the knowledge available at the time, and cannot really be blamed for that.

What is more problematic is the way that his theory largely ignored how those individuals like Gretchen Brandt and Jan Rensaleer, who refused to act against their own consciences when taking part in his experiment, were perfectly capable of engaging in co-operative action. He describes their behaviour, but doesn't develop a theory which can account for it, except by saying that they were in the 'autonomous mode'. But that is to oversimplify the situation. These two people had no objection to going along with anything else in the experiment – indeed, they cooperated willingly in the experiment until the point where it became apparent that harm could result. And even after that, they remained willing to cooperate in other respects: they simply refused to administer any more electric shocks. So to present the agentic or autonomous states as a simple either-or condition in the human being is to oversimplify considerably.

This theory, too, is an attempt to explain social action purely in individual terms. It sees what people do as arising purely from the characteristics of the individual, and again that ignores the reality of social life. To see obedience as an internal, inherited state is to ignore the way that children are systematically socialised into obedience – and for a child, the consequences of not being obedient are very serious indeed. You try being a 7-year-old and openly defying your teacher! Whether you are in a strict disciplinarian school or not, the behaviour will set off a chain reaction of consequences likely to ensure that you will only do it in very extreme circumstances, and probably never again.

What I am trying to say is that there are very real power relationships in society. Out there, as the saying goes, the bastards are using live ammunition. If the soldiers at My Lai had refused to obey orders, they would have been up on a charge of mutiny, or whatever the army equivalent is. It wouldn't matter in the slightest whether society as a whole judged them as being right, they would still be subjected to army discipline. Indeed, it is highly unlikely that society as a whole would ever have heard of it. And army discipline, if you think of it, is by necessity designed to make soldiers more frightened of disobeying orders than they are of being killed. Otherwise, soldiers would simply obey basic survival impulses and run away. To attempt to explain obedience in individual terms, without looking at the very real power relationships in society, is to ignore what is really going on. A theory of obedience which ignores that kind of issue can't possibly present an adequate explanation for the phenomenon.

Traditional approaches to social psychology, then, suffer from several problems. One is that they ignore questions of how social experience changes over time, as we saw when we were looking at research into impression formation and attraction. Another is that they ignore questions of social purpose – what the behaviour or processes are actually used for, as we saw when looking at research into non-verbal communication and attribution. And the third is that they are reductionist – they try to explain social behaviour purely in terms of the individuals concerned, and ignore the wider social and political context of social experience, as we saw in the theories of social impact and social agency. To attempt to explain bystander intervention, crowd behaviour or obedience without

looking at the wider social beliefs and power relationships of
society is simply naïve.

European social psychology

The revolution going on in social psychology is all about responding to these problems. It began with the development of a new
school of thought in social psychology, which became known as
European social psychology. This distinguished it from the more
traditional form of social psychology, which was very much
American in its orientation. And the reason why it was particularly
associated with Europe is that it grew up among European psychologists. Some of them were working in America, having fled
Nazi Germany, but their ways of thinking were quite different
from that of the more traditional American psychologists.

The main reason for these differences lay partly in everyday
European experiences of multiculturalism, produced by a constant
history of neighbours with different languages, cultural practices
and beliefs; and partly in the lessons of Nazi Germany and the
Second World War. Other psychologists had also tried to explain
what had happened in Europe, but they had tended to adopt individual explanations, such as Adorno *et al.*'s authoritarian personality theory. Although these provided some useful insights into
social prejudice, they simply couldn't explain what had happened
to whole communities during the Nazi era.

For example, Milgram's work gave insight into the widespread
nature of obedience, but despite the fact that 'I was only obeying
orders' was the most popular defence at Nuremberg, this still
wasn't considered to be a sufficient explanation. In Milgram's
experiments, people stopped obeying the minute they thought they
could get away with it: if the experimenter went out of the room,
obedience dropped to near zero. But in Europe, people continued
to act in accordance with the Nazi system whether they were super-
vised or not. Many identified with its basic beliefs, while at the
same time convincing themselves that when the Nazis talked of
Vernichtung – annihilation – of the Jews, they didn't really mean it.

The reality of what was going on was too horrifying for many
to acknowledge, even to themselves. This was true outside
Germany as well as within it. Bruno Bettelheim had been in
Dachau, and was only freed as a result of powerful representations
from the international scientific community. Once out, he wrote a

paper analysing the psychological processes underlying how guards and inmates defined themselves and each other, and how this process became self-fulfilling and self-perpetuating. The paper was turned down by several scientific journals on the grounds that it was 'implausible'. It was eventually published in 1943 in the *Journal of Abnormal and Social Psychology*.

As both Hannah Arendt and Bruno Bettelheim pointed out, most of the Nazis, including well-known ones like Eichmann, were not demons, or even particularly evil people. Arendt's book on Eichmann's trial in Jerusalem was subtitled *A Report on the Banality of Evil*, and that is exactly what it is. It shows how one of the most monstrous crimes against humanity was actually committed by ordinary people, and how everyday mechanisms of ordinary social living allowed it to happen.

In addition to the Nazis, for example, understanding what went on also involved explaining the actions of other members of the European population, such as the elders in the Jewish ghettos, who drew up the lists and without whose co-operation the pogroms would have been impossible; and also the actions of other people, German or not, who acquiesced in what was going on. It also means explaining those who did not, such as the Danish people, whose open refusal to co-operate with the Nazis was the latter's first real encounter with direct, open opposition. They were totally unequipped to deal with it, and acquiesced immediately.

All of this meant that the psychologists of the new school of European Social Psychology knew better than to attempt simplistic, reductionist explanations for social behaviour. Instead, they drew on both sociological and psychological thinking, and studied social behaviour in the contexts of real societies, with real inequalities in power and status, and all the social implications deriving from those. The *European Journal of Social Psychology* was founded in 1972, and became steadily more influential. In terms of British social psychology, it would probably be fair to say that it has now become the dominant paradigm, although you might not think so from many introductory syllabuses.

Theories in European social psychology
Theoretical developments in European Social Psychology were particularly stimulated by the work of Serge Moscovici in France and Henri Tajfel in Britain. The new approach took an interactive stance to social psychology, dealing explicitly with phenomena

such as shared social beliefs and intergroup conflicts, and analysing these on several levels. Being European, with a corresponding awareness of the richness of cultures and languages, European social psychologists ensured that their theories could come to terms with pluralism and diversity, and didn't just reflect the culture and practices of the white middle-class mainstream.

The main way that this was achieved was to emphasise, not phenomena, as traditional social psychology did (choose a social event and then study it), but processes. They tried to identify the underlying social psychological mechanisms which influence how human beings go about social living. The three key theories in this respect are social identity theory, social representation theory, and some of the more recent versions of attribution theory. We will be looking at these more closely in Chapter 7. Together, though, these three theories represent the core of modern European Social Psychology. Doise (1984) argued that social behaviour can be understood using four levels of explanation, encompassed within the European framework. These are:

1   *General ideas about social relations*, such as social representations: shared beliefs about how the world works.
2   *Intergroup levels of explanation*, as in social identity theory.
3   *Interactive levels of explanation*, such as the study of non-verbal communication, relationships, attraction, and so on.
4   *Intra-individual levels of explanation*, such as personal constructs or attributions.

Unlike the old-style individualistic social psychology, European social psychology doesn't discount individual levels of analysis. But, on the other hand, it doesn't claim that those are all that matter, either. Instead, its theories are formulated so that they can link the different levels of explanation. Although any one researcher may be concerned with only one level of investigation, understanding social life depends on seeing it in its social context. It is for this reason that European social psychology has emerged as an alternative to the social reductionism of traditional social psychology.

Chapter 7

European Social Psychology

As we saw in the last chapter, one of the major problems with social psychology, until very recently, has been that it lacked theoretical coherence. Traditional social psychology consists largely of numerous small bits of information, each covering just one or two small facets of social living, and having no connection at all with each other. Although one or two 'themes' can be seen recurring from time to time, such as reinforcement explanations for social events, or social exchange processes, these have been limited in their scope, and have failed to provide general links or overarching theories.

But why do general theories matter? Essentially, because of the diversity of human behaviour. People do all sorts of things, in all sorts of ways, and it would be an impossible task to chart them all separately. Nor could anybody hope to make sense out of all those bits of separate research, even if they were all classified and documented. A specific theory which only explains one or two bits of human behaviour isn't much help to us in understanding the human being. We need theoretical coherence so that we can cope with the unpredictable: so that, faced with a new problem in a new area, we can at least begin to see how we might go about tackling it.

At the same time, any modern theory purporting to explain human behaviour needs to be able to come to terms with pluralism. Society is no longer mono-cultural (if, indeed, it ever was), and the old type of social psychology, which assumed that the values, attitudes and behaviour of white transatlantic undergraduates would be typical of the whole human race is no longer tenable. Increasing pressure from both within and outside psychology is gradually forcing the discipline to include alternative perspectives and the recognition of valid alternatives.

So how are we to reconcile these two needs? On the one hand, we need overarching, integrating theories, and on the other hand, we need to recognise and acknowledge pluralism and diversity.

One possible way of coping with this is to fall back on relativism – we might choose to adopt a general multi-application theory like personal construct theory: seeing all alternatives as equally valid, and looking at how an individual person constructs her reality from the information which she has available. By doing so, we have a theoretical model which can account for why everyone thinks differently.

But constructive alternativism has its problems too – not least of which is the fact that, as the saying goes, out there the bastards are using live ammunition. Explaining social life entirely in terms of the theories which we deduce from our experience can't handle the fact that there are undeniable and serious inequalities of power, wealth and access to resources in society. These inequalities have their influences, both on human behaviour and on the way that we understand our worlds. Some people's versions of reality are backed up with more power than others. It is for that reason that totally relativist explanations are only part of the answer. In an ideal world, they might be the whole answer, but this is not an ideal world, and there are things going on at the sociological, political and economic levels which exert powerful influences on all aspects of experience.

This leads us to the second major problem of traditional social psychology: its reductionism. Essentially, traditional social psychology attempts to explain the social world by looking at the actions of individuals, and assuming that these, combined together, make up social reality. But this ignores other levels of explanation, and because it does so, it cannot come to terms with what else is going on. So, for example, Zimbardo put forward his theory of deindividuation as an explanation for why crowds watching potential suicides on high in the United States chant 'Jump, jump!' Deindividuation, an individual mechanism, is supposed to explain why this happens. But, like so many other reductionist explanations, it actually does nothing of the sort.

For one thing, it doesn't begin to explain why some people don't join in with these crowds while others do, and that is an important question. Until we can understand that, we have little hope of understanding the real psychological processes which are going on. And it also carries no acknowledgement of the cultural specificity of the behaviour. Crowds in other countries don't generally act in this way. Suicides in Europe, for instance, generally undertake the act in private; and in Japan, even if it is done publicly, it is done quickly. Jumping off high buildings in public view appears to be a distinctively American practice. So what is it that is distinctive about the United States of America that provokes this very public form of suicidal behaviour. Deindividuation, or any other reductionist model for that matter, cannot begin to explain any of this.

As with all questions of reductionism, what we come down to is the question of single-level explanations as opposed to interactionism. We saw in Chapter 1 how a reductionist position maintains that just this one level of explanation is all that we need, while an interactionist approach says that human behaviour needs to be understood by looking at it from several levels of explanation. It is the interactionist view which is better fitted to deal with the complexities of human behaviour. Deindividuation may be a factor in the suicide crowd event – indeed, it probably is – but it isn't the whole explanation. There is a lot more to crowd behaviour that needs explaining.

In other, more positive types of crowds, for instance, there is the question of the shared peak experience. My esteemed colleague, Banyard, P., described the transcendent experience of being a member of a football crowd that rose as one and chanted 'You Fat Bastard' as a certain lachrymose player entered the field. I personally recall a similar experience at Silverstone in 1973, when Jackie Stewart spun off and a grandstand full of motor racing fans spontaneously stood up and cheered. The positive experience of being part of such spontaneous and concerted crowd behaviour is one for which traditional social psychology can offer little explanation. Yet for those who take part in it, it offers an experience of commonality and shared perception which is uniquely vivid.

In fact, most of the more social aspects of experience – the feeling of identifying with one's group, of being a member of a team, of representing your professional field – are not readily explained by traditional social psychology. And it is unlikely that they ever will be, while traditional social psychology continues to treat social experience as an individual event, and fails to look at the interaction between society, culture and the individual.

These criticisms of social psychology are not new. Both Durkheim and Wundt talked about the importance of collective beliefs in the understanding of social life, and this theme was continued by McDougall (1920), and later by Sherif. Farr (1984) described how the original study of attitudes included the important dimension of attitudes as shared, social beliefs, resulting in shared ideas and behaviour that were not the same as those produced by the same individuals acting independently. But Floyd Allport (1924), in an approach which typified the mainstream of American social psychology from then on, argued firmly that social psychology was 'a part of the psychology of the individual', and nothing more, and that was the view that stuck. Although individual researchers adopted different approaches from time to time, social psychology as a discipline stayed with the individual-istic approach.

The growth of European social psychology

But events in Europe before, during and after the Second World War showed very clearly that individualistic explanations of social behaviour were simply inadequate. As Hannah Arendt pointed out, most of the Nazis, including well-known ones like Eichmann, were not demons, or particularly evil people. Her book was subti-tled *A Report on the Banality of Evil*, and that is exactly what it shows. And in addition to the Nazis, there was the need to explain the actions of other members of the European population: the actions of the elders in the Jewish ghettos, who drew up the lists and without whose co-operation the pogroms would have been impossible; the actions of other people, German or not, who acquiesced in what was going on. And so on.

Many European psychologists fled to America or Britain. Bruno Bettelheim, for example, escaped from a concentration camp and went to America, but the paper he wrote about his experiences in the camp was largely ignored. Social psychology had neither the theoretical orientation to deal with it, nor the willingness to con-front such unpleasant realities. Slowly, however, this began to change, as psychologists returned to Europe or re-established links with other psychologists there. Psychology gradually began to develop theories which were robust enough to explain the realities of social life. At the beginning of the 1970s, the *European Journal of Social Psychology* was founded, and in 1972, Henri Tajfel published a paper entitled 'Some developments in European social psychology', which began to construct a definite identity for a new approach to social psychology: European social psychology.

European social psychology developed rapidly through the 1970s and 1980s, focused largely on the theoretical work of Serge Moscovici in France and Henri Tajfel in Britain. The new approach

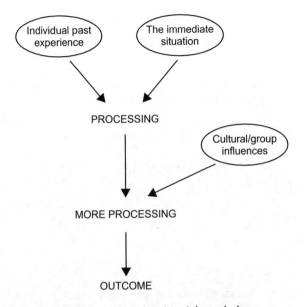

FIGURE 7.1 'American' social psychology

took an interactive stance to social psychology, dealing explicitly with phenomena such as shared social beliefs or intergroup conflict, and working on several levels. Being European, with a corresponding awareness of the richness of cultures and languages, European social psychologists have always been keen to ensure that their theories can come to terms with pluralism and diversity.

The main way that they set out to do this was to emphasise not the study of individual phenomena, as traditional social psychology did (choose a social event and then study it), but social processes. European social psychologists aim to identify the underlying mechanisms which influence how human beings go about social living. As a result of this, the theoretical framework within which research takes place is of paramount importance. Unlike American social psychology, in which theory is seen as an optimal extra to be tacked on later, the theoretical basis of social psychology is core. The three key theories of European social psychology are social representation theory, social identification theory, and some of the more recent formulations of attribution theory.

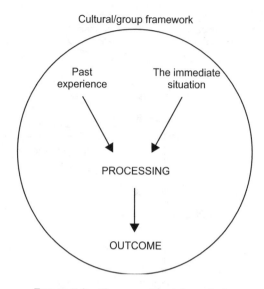

Cultural/group framework

FIGURE 7.2   'European' social psychology

Social representation theory

Social representation theory was developed by Serge Moscovici in France, through the 1960s and 1970s. It is concerned with the shared social beliefs which influence what counts as valid explanation in everyday life. As we know, certain explanations appear to have far more popular acceptance than others: look at how long maternal deprivation theory has survived, or at how psychoanalytic forms of explanation have come to permeate everyday life. Any study of psychology will show how the evidence for these ideas is shaky, to say the least. But that doesn't make them any less popular.

Moscovici argued that it is the shared social representations held by a group or society which allow members of that group to communicate effectively. Social representations make ideas conventional and familiar, and by so doing, they come to guide social action. They can also limit social action if such action involves different groups of people who have different social representations. Di Giacomo (1980) studied the social representations in a student protest movement at a university in Belgium. It turned out that the student leaders held very different social representations from the majority of the students, and these differences meant that in the end, their attempts to rouse the students to action failed. For example, the student leaders spoke of 'student–worker solidarity', but the ordinary students saw 'students' and 'workers' as having very little in common. Effectively, the two groups saw the world differently, and this meant that they couldn't really communicate with one another.

Shared beliefs are powerful social forces, and they influence, directly, what can be done in a given society. In Britain, for instance, any discussion of criminal rehabilitation is likely to come up against the shared social belief that you can't change people. It's a very powerful part of our social belief system, with a very long political and social history. But it isn't shared by other societies. I remember being at a conference on child sexual abuse, and watching an argument between an American friend, who was the director of a rehabilitation unit for teenage sex offenders, and an English professional in the field. The Englishwoman believed firmly that such people would automatically revert to their previous behaviour once the rehabilitation programme was over, whereas the American woman knew, from experience, that it was possible to develop a programme which made a lasting and permanent change. It was a complete clash of social representations, which meant that the two of them were completely unable to communicate.

What we are talking about here is the sociological concept of ideology. One of the fundamental ideological beliefs of American society is that people can change. But one of the fundamental ideological beliefs in British society is that people can't, or at least don't. These beliefs link closely with social structures, the class system, political approaches to crime, and a host of other social phenomena – including theories of intelligence, of which more later.

These are not beliefs which just hang around in the air. They are beliefs which are held by real people, and which are actively used to make sense out of social experience. Moscovici discussed how people negotiate their own versions of social representations, through conversations, and by drawing ideas from the media and fitting them into their own personal construct system, or the schemas which they use to organise their activity in the world around them.

Social representations, then, are the interface between the sociological concept of ideology and an individual's own thinking style.

One of the first studies of social representations was conducted by Moscovici, in 1961, and was concerned with how psychoanalytic concepts had come to be so commonly accepted in French society; and how in becoming so they had become a form of social dogma, providing arbitrary explanations which served to justify social practices – something that was very different from the scientific theory which Freud had originally developed.

Moscovici identified three phases in how the theory had become transformed into a social representation. The first was the scientific phase, in which psychoanalysis was elaborated as a scientific theory, and knowledge of its tenets and practices was largely restricted to professional scientists. This was followed by a second phase, in which the images and concepts of psychoanalysis began to diffuse through society, and were modified or recast in the process. The third phase was described by Moscovici as the ideological phase, in which the transformed version of psychoanalysis came to signify a school of thought, adopted by power bases in society and thus becoming not only accepted, but enforced as a product of thinking.

Social representations, then, are not static: they change with time, and in ways that are directly influenced by other forces in society. Fischler (1980) showed how changes in social representations of what constitutes an acceptable diet reflect social and economic changes, some concerned with the production, distribution and consumption of food, and others concerned with the adoption of new, consumer-based lifestyles which involve different modes of eating, in the sense of the increased emphasis on fast food and snacks rather than meals. Jodelet (1984) described a study of changes in social representations of the body, in terms of the influence of youth movements, women's liberation and other social factors.

The theoretical basis for understanding these changes is to see social representations as having a consistent central nucleus, which doesn't change, surrounded by peripheral elements, which do. You can see this if you look at ideas about education in this country. The consistent central nucleus here would be the idea that some people just can't be taught. That belief can be seen as inherently ideological, linking directly with the British class system. However, the theories which have been used to justify that central nucleus – the peripheral elements – have changed over time. At first, it was the genetic theory of intelligence, then it was the Piagetian idea of biological 'readiness', and then it was social deprivation. But the end result was the same – the overriding idea that some kids would never be able to achieve anything in education. The central core stayed the same while the peripheral elements changed – and the wealth of scientific and social evidence which directly challenged it was simply dismissed or ignored.

Social representation theory, then, provides us with a framework within which ideology, shared beliefs and individual social cognition can be linked. It lets us study social cognition in the real context of when and where it happens, and what social purposes it serves. The study of social representations is well-developed in many European countries, although the theory has been relatively little known in the UK. But that is rapidly changing, as interest in shared social beliefs begins to grow.

Social identity theory

Social identity theory is perhaps the most influential of all of the European social psychology theories. It has been applied in a number of different contexts, such as explanations of prejudice or aspects of the self-concept. And it is the way that it can be applied to so many different phenomena in social psychology which indicates how very different it is from most of the traditional theories.

Hogg and Abrams (1988) showed how the theory doesn't invalidate the earlier findings of social psychologists. Instead, it sets them into context. In their book, they showed how the results of classic studies can be reinterpreted as manifestations of social identity, and how doing so helps us to make sense in explaining why people act as they do in those particular contexts. In many ways, social identity theory takes up Sherif's work on social norms and conformity, and provides a framework within which the observations and findings link into a coherent social pattern, which takes account of real-world pressures as well as individual cognitions.

Social identity theory, as expressed by Tajfel and Turner (1979), argues that personal identity can be located on a continuum, ranging from purely individual identity at one end to purely social identity at the other. We all belong to a number of social groups, and these are part of how we think about ourselves. When I speak as a psychologist, I am not just playing a role: my being a psychologist is part of me, and I can become very defensive if my social group is disparaged by an 'outsider' – even though I might spend a lot of my own time criticising psychology! I don't identify as a psychologist all of the time, of course – there are individual aspects of my self-concept as well, and other social identities – but when the occasion demands, it will come to the fore.

Social identity, as opposed to personal identity, becomes strongest when circumstances make it relevant to the immediate situation. So we may shift from personal to social identity, even during a single conversation, if social identity becomes salient. An argument about who does the washing-up may shift from being an interpersonal one to an intergroup conflict if gender becomes a salient issue. It depends what appears relevant at the time.

More importantly, though, social identity theory allows us to see social groups in their wider context. The theory emphasises how real social groups differ from one another in terms of power and status, and how those differences, in turn, affect how people belonging to those groups behave. People need to feel that belonging to their own group is a positive thing, so, if they belong to a group which is inferior in social status, they will try to change the status of that group, or compare themselves with other, inferior groups, or engage in a number of other mechanisms to make it bearable.

Failing that, they will try to leave, or dissociate themselves from the group. The controversy over Michael Jackson's supposed 'skin disorder' was directly about whether he was attempting to dissociate himself from a group which he personally perceived as inferior, at a time when others were challenging the whole idea of the group as inferior. He said not, but the evidence of his other cosmetic changes went against him.

There are three fundamental processes in social identification. The first of these is categorisation: the basic human tendency to classify experience into groups. We do this with inanimate objects and animals as well as with people. The second of these processes is social comparison: our tendency to compare one group of people with another. And the third of these is the human drive to seek sources of positive self-esteem. Putting these three underlying mechanisms together results in social identification.

There are a great many implications which spring from this apparently straightforward model. One of them is the way that even the basic process of categorising people and things seems to make people perceive them as being more different from one another. It even applies to judgements about lengths of lines (Tajfel and Wilkes, 1963), and is even stronger when we are talking about social groups.

For instance, in a study in which white Canadians or Indians were asked to speak to an audience, Doise, Deschamps and Meyer (1978) found that people accentuated those aspects of the speakers' behaviour which fitted with their stereotypes but not those which were non-stereotypical. It has been known for a long time that highly prejudiced individuals are more likely to perceive extreme racial differences than other people. Because they see the world as sharply categorised, that exaggerates their perceptions. So the process of social categorisation, in itself, can exaggerate group discrimination.

The process of social comparison involves applying a broader social knowledge to the categorisations that we make. It brings in our own world-knowledge, our social representations, and, most importantly, the views of other people who we regard as similar to ourselves. Essentially, it is about evaluating other groups: weighing them up in terms of their place in the world. But in doing so, we gather social knowledge and ideas from members of our own group, because we see them as being like ourselves. So in the end, there is a tendency for their views to be seen as being more 'true' than other views. For the most part, we favour the beliefs of the social groups that we identify with – a process which links inextricably with the development of social representations.

We also weigh up social groups in terms of their relative social status. So, for example, in a study comparing student perceptions of universities, Spears and Manstead (1989) found that students from Manchester and Exeter Universities were more inclined to compare themselves with students from Oxford University than with students from what was then Manchester Polytechnic. This comparison led them to exaggerate the differences between themselves and polytechnic students, and to ignore the similarities.

This links with the third process, which is the question of self-esteem. Identification with a social group means that membership of that group becomes incorporated into the self-concept. The students in the Spears and Manstead study had an incentive for comparing themselves with Oxford University students, since the latter were seen as having higher social prestige. The distancing from the polytechnic students was also self-serving, since they saw polytechnic students as having lower social status.

Social identity theory, then, allows us to see social interaction in terms of how the behaviour of the individual human being links with the wider social realities. It tackles, directly, the question of in-groups and out-groups in society, and shows how the 'them-and-us' issues which are so much a part of human psychology in the real world come about.

Attribution theory

Within the European context, attribution theory underwent a dramatic change of emphasis, becoming much more concerned with analysing the nature of everyday explanations. The traditionally detached views of how people make attributions, such as Kelley's covariance theory, have been criticised (for example, by Lalljee, 1981) because they assume that we make an entirely new attribution each time. They use a computer analogy, assuming that the human being processes information in a way similar to that of a computer. But, as we will see in Chapter 9, human cognition is very different from computer information processing, and draws on much wider social awareness. In the same way, our everyday attributions incorporate our social knowledge, our social representations and our social identifications too. They don't just happen in a context-free manner.

As a result of this, there has been a growing interest in how attribution and explanation are used in intergroup situations. For example, Taylor and Jaggi (1974) compared the attributions made by Hindu and Muslim groups in Southern India about themselves and each other. They found that people tended to make more internal attributions for socially desirable behaviour by members of their own groups, but used external attributions to explain socially desirable behaviour from the others. In other words, their own group acted positively because they were nice people, while the other group acted positively because they couldn't help it – the situation made them do so. It was, of course, the other way round when the behaviour being explained was socially undesirable. This way of exploring how conflicting groups in social identity terms perceive each other can tell us a great deal about how conflicts become self-perpetuating, and can last over many generations.

Attribution theory has also been used to throw light on how social representations develop. For example, Moscovici and Hewstone (1983) used attributional analysis to show how split-brain research became transformed from a scientific theory into a social representation. Most introductory psychology students are familiar with the scientific evidence on split-brain studies, and aware that this simply shows that language, mathematical and spatial abilities seem to be partially localised in different cerebral hemispheres. But Moscovici and Hewstone showed how that research has become transformed into a social belief that: (a) the two halves of the brain are two different, independent minds; (b) that each deals exclusively with opposing skills; (c) that these include major aspects of personality, for example, intuition, masculinity and so on; and (d) that this explains social differences, because society favours those with left-hemisphere dominance.

In other words, the scientific evidence that the two hemispheres tend to mediate slightly different cognitive skills has become completely changed, shifting from a description of a few experimental phenomena to an ideological explanation for why society is like it is. This was even extended by some people to include technology, wars, and repressive authoritarian social practices. Since social representations are all about how we make sense of the world, looking at the group-based attributions which people make can help us to make connections between individual explanations and the wider social representations of society.

This principle can be applied to smaller groups too. For example, some of my own research uses attributional analysis to identify social representations. This is useful in looking at managerial beliefs, and how they lead to organisational practices which can foster or damage positive social identifications at work (Hayes, 1991). But this type of attribution theory is very different from the information-processing model implicit in covariance or correspondent inference theory.

Together, then, these three theories represent the core of modern European social psychology. They provide us with overarching theories which allow us to re-evaluate a great deal of existing research in social psychology, and to offer theoretical frameworks and explanations which deal with a much richer portion of the social fabric.

One of the reasons why this is possible is because they link together several different levels of explanation. As we saw in Chapter 6, Doise (1984) identified four levels of explanation within which these theoretical developments could be understood, ranging from general ideas about social relations to individual cognitive mechanisms. The increasing use of these different levels of explanation, and the development of complementary theories at each of these levels, has resulted in European social psychology forming a kind of 'meta-theory' within which social psychology is being re-evaluated and re-conceptualised.

The aim of European social psychology is not to seek to explain everything in individualistic psychological terms; but nor is it to say that our entire experience is socially determined. There is also personal identity and individual belief. But what it does try to do is to develop theories which will link the different levels of explanation, by focusing on underlying social psychological mechanisms. It also seeks theories which can come to terms with pluralism, new situations and new problems. By doing so, it is revolutionising our view of social psychology.

Chapter 8

The Child's Social World

The concept of individuality is one which has been a powerful influence in Western thinking since the time of the ancient Greeks. Both philosophers and psychologists have attempted to understand the human being as if it were an independent, entirely separate agent, developing as a result of internal genetic imperatives and only connected with other people through instrumental ties.

But this is entirely unrealistic. People are not just individuals, although of course we all have our own individual experiences, ideas and thoughts. People are embedded in their social networks. We grow up surrounded by people, we learn from other people, and we are genetically predisposed to develop attachments with other people. The fact that the human being is a *social* animal shapes both our cognitions and our cognitive development, very much more than we realise. But it is only relatively recently that psychologists have been realising just how very deeply social human beings actually are.

That realisation is developing in a number of different areas. The previous two chapters showed how it has emerged in European social psychology and its related theories. In the next chapter we will be looking at the ways that even cognitive processing is powerfully influenced by social contexts and implications. But it is perhaps in our psychological understanding of the child's cognitive development that it has become most apparent. In the rest of this chapter, we will explore some of the psychological evidence which has illustrated just how very much more complex the child's social understanding is than earlier psychologists had ever imagined.

Piaget and cognitive development

For much of the twentieth century, our psychological understanding of the child's cognitive development was dominated by the Piagetian model. The influence of this theory was so strong that for several decades, research into cognitive development operated entirely within its framework, and there was very little investigation of alternative approaches. But since the 1980s, a growing body of research into social factors in the child's cognitive development has become apparent.

As far as Piaget was concerned, cognitive development occurred primarily through the reduction of egocentricity. The infant's first major cognitive task was to interpret sensory information and learn motor coordination, which would eventually lead the child to differentiate between 'me' and 'not-me' – that is, between itself and the outside world. Piaget believed that this differentiation begins with the acquisition of object constancy, and becomes gradually stronger from then on. But the complete separation of 'me' from 'not-me' – in other words, the full reduction of egocentricity – comes when the child finally achieves adult-style thought processes. The various stages of thinking outlined by Piagetian theory – both the stages of cognitive development and the stages of moral development – reflect the degree to which egocentricity has been reduced.

Problems of Piagetian theory

Piaget's model was very plausible, and widely accepted. But there were a number of problems with it, which became more apparent as the century progressed. Some of these were methodological in nature. Researchers exploring different ways of presenting Piagetian tasks found that framing the task in a familiar context, or conducting it in such a way that it did not inadvertently lead the child into the wrong answer, made a tremendous difference to the outcomes. Children might be egocentric, but they were evidently far more cognitively capable than the pure Piagetian approach implied.

Other research highlighted the importance of social interaction in the child's development. Attachment studies, particularly those investigating attachment in the child's own home, showed how infants are sociable and engaged in interaction with others from their earliest days, and also showed how these interactions formed the basis of later attachment. Infant 'pre-programming' all pointed to a highly sociable infant whose main source of learning was other people – an approach which clashed directly with the Piagetian perspective.

Studies of feral children, such as Genie and the Koluchova twins, showed that social contact makes all the difference to cognitive development; and language development studies such as the study of the deaf child Jim by Bard and Sachs (1977) showed how human interaction as well as exposure to spoken language is necessary if a child is to acquire full language functioning.

Overall, these challenges to traditional Piagetian theory indicated a growing interest in social influences and the way they affect cognitive development. Researchers began to investigate cognitive development in its social context; and as they did so, they discovered that the child's understanding was far more sophisticated than had previously been believed. Within their own familiar environments, they demonstrated an intriguing level of social and cognitive competence.

Family interactions

Family interactions are a central part of the young child's world, and they form a rich social context within which the child develops. Through family interaction, the child is able to develop its world-knowledge and its awareness of what counts as acceptable or unacceptable behaviour. The emotions and conflicts of family life, as well as the play and humour, are also crucial features of the way that the child learns. Socio-cognitive development is not just a matter of responding to demands or sanctions and learning to act in accordance with them. It involves active intentions, emotions and dynamic exchanges.

This was demonstrated very clearly in a research project which was carried out in Cambridge by Judy Dunn. The project involved a longitudinal, ethological study of pre-school children in 52 families, from a variety of socio-economic backgrounds. The observers in the studies tried to be as unobtrusive as possible; although, of course, it would be unrealistic to think that they had no effect at all on the way that the families behaved. But the same researchers visited the family each time, so that the children (and parents) could get used to them, and they visited quite often. Also, although they didn't interrupt or interfere, the observers did try to be as natural as possible, so they would respond if a child spoke to them rather than remaining silent.

What emerged was a direct challenge to the assumptions about children's cognitive, and moral, development made by earlier researchers. Dunn and her colleagues found that even from 18 months of age, children understood a variety of interpersonal and moral issues, which would not have been comprehensible if the child were as egocentric as had been assumed. Although they were unable to express this understanding by responding to a hypothetical problem set by an experimenter – the way that traditional Piagetian research was carried out – the nature of their interaction within the family showed that even very young children possessed, and used, quite complex social understanding.

There were four features of this understanding which emerged particularly clearly in the study. These were: understanding other people's feelings, understanding other people's goals, understanding social rules, and understanding other minds.

Understanding others' feelings
Researchers into infant behaviour had often observed how even very young children seem to 'tune in' to the moods of others, responding to distress, amusement or happiness. Dunn found that children are deeply interested in emotional states, and their understanding of them develops throughout the second and third years of age. For example, in one case an 18-month-old child was watching its older sibling crying bitterly while lying face-down on its mother's knee. The child was looking serious, and the mother asked him what was wrong with his sister. The child, with a concerned expression, bent down, turned his head to look at his sister face to face, and stroked her hair.

Understanding other people's feelings, though, doesn't necessarily mean sparing them. As most mothers rapidly discover, small children often take a great delight in teasing or upsetting their siblings. Although the children in the study clearly understood distress, they might respond in any one of five ways: ignoring, watching, trying to comfort, laughing, or acting to make things worse. Dunn found that age had a great deal to do with this: children closer to 36 months were more likely to comfort their siblings, particularly if they had not caused the distress in the first place, than children of 18 or 24 months.

Understanding others' goals
Very early on, children appear to develop an understanding of other people's intentions or goals. They can co-operate in play with siblings from quite an early age, which requires an understanding of intentions as well as some sensitivity to the other person – both apparently impossible in Piagetian terms at this age.

Even baby games such as 'peek-a-boo' and 'hide-and-seek' involved sustained coordinated interaction, but children's understanding of what other people intend to do often goes way beyond mere repetition. In one example, for example, when an older child began to sing, its 14-month-old sibling went straight to the toybox, searched, and brought out two toys: a music pipe and bells. Then the child held out the pipe to its sibling and made a 'blow' gesture with its lips. In another example, an older sibling was acting out a fairy story with puppets. The child watched, laughing, and then went to the shelf, found other puppets (appropriate to the story) and brought them to its sibling.

Understanding social rules
Interaction with other members of the family – not just the mother, but also with siblings – also produces an increasingly sophisticated knowledge of what is and is not permitted, including when rules will or won't apply, the idea of responsibility, and the use of excuses and justifications. In other words, children of this age don't just learn social rules: they also learn to use them, and even to manipulate them for their own ends. But they learn them as practical knowledge, used within the family. Identifying abstract principles in Piagetian-type clinical interviews is something quite different.

The results of Piagetian studies implied that young children were unable to grasp social rules and principles. But Dunn found that the child's ability to understand and use social rules actually develops steadily throughout the third year of life, until by the time they reach two and a half, or three years of age, children are demonstrating a sophisticated awareness of rules, authority and responsibility.

Understanding social rules, though, isn't the same as obeying them. In part, the children's understanding of the rules was evidenced by the way they used them: taking great delight in pretending to break rules in joint play with their siblings; putting the blame on other people – as in the case of a 30-month-old child who instantly blamed its sister for playing with a hosepipe (previously forbidden by mother), when it had been the child herself who had set the hose off again. Other examples include challenging mother's authority by applying the rule to her as well, as in the case of a 3-year-old child about to play at cooking, who responded to being asked to wash hands by asking why mother didn't wash her hands as well.

Perhaps one of the most significant findings which emerged from Dunn's research was how quickly children learn about rules when the context has some emotional significance for them. At 18 months, children have developed a strong idea of their own rights, and become extremely angry and emotional when they feel these are being infringed. By the age of 36 months, the tantrums have died down somewhat, but they are much more inclined to argue and dispute – often about the same issues.

Dunn argues that the role of emotional involvement in socio-cognitive development has been seriously overlooked; and it may provide an important key to understanding both the motivation and the mechanism for the child's developing cognitive awareness.

Understanding other minds

Another thing that emerged from the Cambridge studies was the young child's growing awareness of other people's minds and their moods. This observation links very closely with another area of research into children's socio-cognitive development: research into the child's 'theory of mind'.

One of the classic studies which demonstrated the way that children develop a 'theory of mind' was carried out by Wimmer and Perner, in 1983. It involved acting out a story for the children, using dolls and toys. In the story, Sally comes into a room and puts a marble into a basket. Then she goes outside. Anne comes into the room, sees the marble, and hides it in her own box, which is also in the room. Then Anne goes out. After that, Sally comes back to look for her marble. At this point, the children were asked three questions. The first was: 'Where is the marble now?' And the second was 'Where was the marble in the beginning?' These two were included to make sure that the children had really followed what was going on. But the real test question was: 'Where will Sally look for her marble?'

What Wimmer and Perner found was that there were distinct age differences in the answer to this question. Children of four and upwards had no problem: they could understand that Sally would believe something that was not longer true, and look for her marble in the place where she had left it. But 3-year-olds tended to say that Sally would look in the box, not realising that she would not know that it had been moved.

This finding confirms a number of other studies in this area, and implies that a full 'awareness of mind' – that is, an understanding that other people's thinking is not the same as one's own – comes into play at about three-and-a-half years of age.

The fact that a theory of mind appears to have developed by four years old, though, doesn't mean that it comes into being full-blown. Children continue to develop their understanding, and their theories of mind become more sophisticated as they grow older. For example, Harris *et al.* (1986) told children stories about situations where a character might want to hide how they felt. In one story, for instance, the central character had a tummy ache, but wanted to go outside and play; he tried to hide his tummy ache, because he knew that his mother would stop him from going out if he told her about it.

All the children understood what the boy's real feelings would be. But the 4-year-olds found it difficult to describe what he would pretend to feel, and how other people would interpret it. The 6-year-olds, on the other hand, were able to predict the boy's behaviour, and also realised that adults would be likely to be misled by it. So the 4-year-olds had developed a theory of mind, in that they were able to understand one other person's point of view, but the 6-year-olds were more sophisticated, and able to appreciate more than one person's point of view simultaneously.

Another aspect of having a theory of mind is that one becomes able to appreciate the difference between a lie and a false belief. In one study, Wimmer, Gruber and Perner (1984) told children a story, again acting it out using toys and dolls. There were three characters: an older girl, a younger girl and a young boy. They were walking past a wall, and the older girl could see that there was a lion on the other side. The younger girl could only see the lion's tail, and asked the older girl what it was. The older girl said that it was a dog. Then the young boy asked the younger girl what it was, and she told him that it was a dog.

When the researchers asked the children about this story, all of them realised that the younger girl had held a false belief. They were clearly aware of the intentions of both the older and the younger girls. But even though they knew that the younger girl did not intend to deceive the boy, the 4-year-olds still judged that the younger girl had lied. Most of the 6-year-olds, on the other hand, did not think that she had lied (although a few of them did). When the researchers put the same problem to 8-year-olds, though, they were very clear: the older girl had lied, because she had intended to deceive; whereas the younger girl had not lied, but had merely expressed a false belief.

What all of these studies about children's theories of mind show us is that the child's social understanding is much more sophisticated than earlier theorists had perceived. From a very early age, children have the social awareness which supports the later development of a theory of mind. The theory of mind itself appears sometime between age three and four; and that form of social understanding continues to become increasingly sophisticated and complex throughout childhood.

Vygotsky's theory of development

So how are we to make sense of these findings? The modern picture is a far cry from the Piagetian image of the egocentric child, struggling to make cognitive sense of its world through problem-solving and rules. Shaffer, Stern, Donaldson, Dunn, Harris, Perner and a host of others have all shown that when it comes to interpreting social situations, the child is infinitely more capable than it appears to be when presented with physical or abstract puzzles.

Making sense of all this requires a perspective on child development which can take into account the interaction between the individual and society, and the way that the child's social life provides the basis for, and amplifies, its cognitive development. This type of perspective can be found in the work of the Russian child psychologist Vygotsky, a Russian psychologist of the 1920s, whose work only became available to the West in the 1960s. In recent years, Vygotskyan perspectives have become extremely popular among modern researchers into child development.

Vygotsky's main emphasis was on the way that culture influences the course of human development. For many Western theorists, including Piaget, organic maturation was seen as the prime motive power for development. But as far as Vygotsky was concerned, organic maturation was a condition rather than a motive power for cultural development. Of course the child requires the biological maturity to be able to achieve certain levels of development; but in Vygotsky's model, it is the child's culture, expressed through social interaction and language, which provides the motivation for that development to happen. Both intellectual and socio-cognitive development require social interaction, social demands and social stimulation if they are to take place. And the child, as we have seen, is powerfully predisposed to engage in that social interaction and to respond to those social demands.

The zone of proximal development

One of the central concepts in Vygotsky's model of development is that of the zone of proximal development. Essentially, the ZPD, as it is often known, is all about the difference between what the child can manage on its own, and what it can achieve when it has help and guidance from other people. Bruner, in his introduction to Vygotsky's book *Thought and Language*, described it as 'scaffolding', which supports the child as it develops cognitive skills and understanding.

Parents, siblings and others all interact socially with children, and children learn to respond appropriately in those interactions. This involves a considerable amount of learning: sometimes from people explaining things or stating rules; sometimes from others amplifying their statements or making games a little more elaborate; and sometimes from sanctions or rewards which communicate social expectations to the child. All this is 'scaffolding' for the child's developing understanding.

What Vygotsky was saying, then, is that what the child achieves on its own, without social interaction, is essentially a basic, 'primitive'

FIGURE 8.1   Vygotsky showed how adults provide structure for children's learning

Source: Photograph by Miranda Brauns.

form of knowledge which allows it to survive in the material world, but not to understand general principles or abstract concepts. But there is also a wide area of potential development which is stimulated by social interaction and language: the zone of proximal development. The child's readiness to respond to other people also makes it ready to learn from that interaction. And learning from that interaction ultimately involves developing sophisticated social knowledge, cognitive skills and abstract reasoning.

Vygotsky's theory, then, allows us to make sense out of a great deal of modern developmental psychology – which is, of course, why modern developmental psychologists have shown so much interest in it! Using this model, we can understand modern language acquisition studies, which emphasise the importance of human social interaction; we can make sense of the accounts of feral or severely deprived children, reared without human contact, and see why those children were like they were when discovered; and we can understand why converting Piagetian studies into contexts which are socially meaningful for children can make so much difference to their cognitive abilities.

This whole paradigm shift is congruent with a much greater trend within modern psychology. In almost all areas of the discipline, we find a growing recognition that the human being is a far more complicated organism than used to be thought. Moreover, people are deeply embedded in their social contexts, and these social contexts are active from their very earliest days. Any understanding of how children develop mentally needs to be firmly rooted in an understanding of the ways that social contexts and social interactions influence a child who is already, from its very earliest days, predisposed towards sociability. Treating the child as if it were an independent individual, entirely separate from its social context, is quite simply unrealistic, and can only give us a distorted picture of what is really going on.

Chapter 9

Perspectives in Cognitive Psychology

When the 'cognitive revolution' of the 1960s and 1970s took place, psychology breathed a metaphorical sigh of relief. For many years, it had been dominated by the rigid demands of behaviourism, with an insistence on an 'objective' approach that many felt had become increasingly trivialised, not least in view of its emphasis on animal learning as the essence of psychological mechanisms.

Like any paradigm change, the cognitive revolution took time to gather momentum. Behaviourism was unquestionably the dominant paradigm in the 1950s, but gradually through the 1960s more and more research in the cognitive field began to trickle through. The 1970s saw the trickle become a flood, and the 1980s saw academic psychology inundated with cognitive psychology – even leading to the development of a whole new discipline: cognitive science.

But the 1980s saw something else too. It saw a gradual emergence of a new interest in cognitive processes developing within other areas of psychology. This took several forms: an increasing amount of research into social beliefs and ideas in social psychology; an increasing interest in how social cognition develops in children; the development of cognitive therapy in clinical psychology; and even the publication of textbooks on animal cognition within the comparative field. These new approachses did not call themselves cognitive psychology, partly because they were dismissed as not being 'real' cognitive psychology by the cognitive psychologists, but partly also because they had little in common with what had by then become 'traditional' cognitive psychology – the formal, laboratory-based search for models of how information is processed. The paradigm shift from behaviourism to cognitive psychology had hardly been achieved before a new paradigm shift had begun. So why did cognitive psychology prove so inadequate?

In many ways, cognitive psychology could claim to have originated with psychology itself. Cognitive topics such as attention, mind and memory were certainly the focus of interest of the early experimental philosophers, and of the introspectionists such as William James or Wilhelm Wundt. But the advent of the behaviourists discredited the study of the 'mind', and their insistence on a rigid methodology and adherence to behaviourist principles meant that during the first half of the twentieth century, psychology's focus moved away from cognition and on to strictly observable forms of behaviour – or the psychometric industry.

At its peak in the 1950s, the dominance of behaviourism was producing a number of reactions. At this time, the foundations of the humanistic school of psychology emerged, through the work of Maslow and Rogers, to gain in influence through the subsequent decades. In the clinical field, George Kelly produced his theory of personal constructs in an attempt to come to terms with the differences in how patients saw their worlds. Kelly's constructive alternativism suggested that cognitions, rather than arising as a rather unimportant by-product of behaviour, were the major factors in determining action. Since people construe different events according to their different personal theories, their responses to those events vary according to the personal constructs that they used. In other words, cognitions determine behaviour.

At the same time, other developments were taking place in the academic world. It had become apparent during the Second World War that the military needed to have a better understanding of how such cognitive processes as attention worked, given the increase in technological complexity which had occurred. There was a military necessity to know, for instance, just how long someone could sit in front of a radar screen without making mistakes; or just how the many dials in an aircraft cockpit should be arranged so that the pilot would be less likely to make fatal errors. Since these were military questions, they received large amounts of funding, and soon research into this was proceeding apace.

It was helped, too, by the discovery that it was possible to study cognitive processes without resorting to introspection, which by now had been thoroughly discredited as a research tool. By operationalising the topic to be studied, researchers became able to use more objective measures. So, for instance, by asking research participants to press a key whenever they noticed a particular signal, it was possible to establish whether they were paying attention to the stimulus or not.

Perhaps the most persuasive arguments promoting the new development of cognitive psychology and the challenges which it offered to behaviourism, however, arose from the work of J. S. Bruner, who showed how human factors like expectation, language, values and the like exerted their influence on what people perceived. Working within a 'scientific' laboratory context, these findings could not be dismissed academically in the same way as those of the humanists (who had largely worked as clinical psychologists), and they showed that an understanding of the active basis of cognition is essential to an understanding of what is going on in people's minds. But Bruner was working before the age of the computer.

Two traditions within cognitive psychology

There have always been two entirely different traditions of research within cognitive psychology. One of these originates within the experimental philosophy tradition, and remained alive and well in the universities throughout the behaviourist era. It dates back to Herman Ebbinghaus (1885).

Ebbinghaus established a tradition of rigorous experimental research into memory, in which the goal was to ensure that only 'pure' memory would be studied. This involved memorising nonsense syllables in order to avoid 'contamination' from extraneous variables such as interest, motivation or, worse still, prior knowledge. It systematised a laboratory research tradition which continues, albeit in modified form, even to the present day, in which the aim is to ensure that the topic under study is as decontextualised and uncontaminated by experience as possible.

That this was – and remains – the dominant paradigm in psychology can be seen in the language with which it is described. Notice the hidden metaphor in the use of the word 'contaminated' – as in 'contaminating variable', or 'our results were contaminated by some of our subjects having had relevant previous experience'. In other words, research which deals with the real world is 'unhygienic' – and therefore to be avoided. The ideal situation is 'sterile', or 'pure'. This is the research paradigm into which students of psychology are first inducted: it is held up as an ideal, and encourages the student to discount real-world experience as somehow invalid. More about this later.

The second tradition in cognitive research, however, while still at times operating within a laboratory context, is much more at ease with real-life experience. In terms of a 'founding father', it can be said to have originated with the work of Bartlett (1932), who investigated among other things the phenomenon of serial learning, and the distortions which occur when the individual is asked to recall or translate meaningful information. Most psychology students are familiar with the way that Bartlett used an Indian 'ghost' story to show how people's conceptions of what the world is like exert a powerful influence on the material which they recall. Other eminent researchers, most notably Bruner and Neisser, have kept this other tradition alive within cognitive psychology – alive, but underemphasised.

Left to themselves, the two traditions might have coexisted and interacted with one another fruitfully. But they were not left to themselves, because science always occurs within a social context. That context included both the rise of the 'expert culture' in society, and the vehement insistence of the behaviourists that psychology must be 'scientific' and that this meant modelling itself on the physical sciences (see Chapter 2). As a result, an ideal emerged in which highly controlled research investigating single-variable causes was seen as being somehow 'better' than other forms of investigation. Since research in the Ebbinghaus tradition fitted this ideal far more readily than the work of Bartlett and his followers, the Ebbinghaus tradition received far more emphasis (and research funding) than the Bartlett one.

One of the reasons for this is that a human cognitive psychology requires a rather different approach to the subject matter. If, as Bartlett showed, it is the sense which people make out of their material which is crucially important in determining how they will deal with it, then we need to come to terms with how people make sense out of things before we can fully understand what is going on. This moves us into the realms of understanding meaning – the realm which the sociologists call hermeneutics. And that is something which makes psychologists who adhere to traditional forms of research methodology feel very uncomfortable indeed. After all, it goes against all of their early socialisation. So cognitive psychologists in general – with some notable exceptions – have tended to avoid such tricky questions and focus on research following the Ebbinghaus tradition.

That doesn't mean, of course, that cognitive research has never been able to deal with personal values or other issues. On the contrary: some of our 'classic' studies in cognitive psychology have done just that. But for many modern cognitive psychologists, the challenges thrown up by the work of, say, Bruner and Neisser, while respected, tend to be respected at a distance. And in the meantime, research in the laboratory tradition continues, with ever more complex information-processing models being developed, and usually at the expense of models which can integrate the social and personal contexts of what is actually happening.

Cognitive psychology and the computer metaphor

One of the reasons for this lies in the forms of explanation which are adopted within the discipline of cognitive psychology. Much of what I shall refer to as 'mainstream' cognitive psychology rests on the computer metaphor, in which the human being is seen as 'like' a computer – in other words, as being effectively a complex information processor. In this type of model (for example, Baddeley, 1983), information is received through the senses, channelled through various filters and processors where it is sorted, allocated to stores and boxes, and then (sometimes) outputted in the form of behaviour being studied.

One of the consequences of this is that mainstream cognitive psychology is full of flow charts and other kinds of mechanical models. The flow charts have a distinct family resemblance to computer diagrams. Uncertainties or 'woolly' concepts like context or background are often relegated to a single inputting box with an arrow feeding into the process somewhere (for example, 'cultural factors'). The emphasis is entirely on the inferred information processing which is happening within the brain.

The problem is that none of this actually gets to the meaning of what is going on. If we look at the process of understanding speech, for instance, we can develop models which involve 'dictionary units' or 'logogens' which identify words; but that doesn't tell us what is going on when we listen to people talking. If I were giving this paper as a lecture to a group of students, and I got this far and then said: 'OK, we've cancelled the rest of this talk, you can have an early lunch now', there would be huge dimensions of meaning which couldn't be addressed by an information-processing metaphor.

Just think for a moment about the complexities of what would happen if I really did say that. How would the students feel? Pleased, I've no doubt, at being let off so lightly. Relieved to be able to move about, rather than sitting still. But maybe a bit cheated too, because I wouldn't really have lived up to the informal 'social contract' which was going on between us. Slightly anxious perhaps as to how what I had covered so far could be converted into an exam answer; and probably rather puzzled, because the behaviour certainly wouldn't live up to the 'script' which we all share about what type of behaviour is expected and appropriate in this sort of situation. None of this can really be expressed by a single box with an arrow (or even three boxes with arrows). In other words, if we really want to understand what human beings say to one another, we need much more than an information-processing flow chart.

In a situation like the one that I've just described, although there would be processing of the information, and the students' brains would be identifying distinct words and so on, that wouldn't tell us the whole story of what is going on. There is more happening, which needs to be explored using other levels of explanation. I am not saying, in any sense, that research into language processing is a total waste of time – it can give us some insight, of course. But I am saying that its value is severely limited, unless it can be integrated with other levels of understanding. We cannot assume that the cognitive perspective alone gives us a full understanding of the human mind.

In part, this has only become a problem because cognitive psychology has committed the same error as that of the behaviourists. Both schools of thought became so seduced by the metaphor which they used to describe their approach that they eventually took the metaphor itself to be the be-all and end-all of understanding what people do. In the case of the behaviourists, it was the idea of the atom and the molecule: the S–R link as the 'atom', which could be combined through increasingly complex learning until it could eventually account for all human behaviour. In the case of cognitive psychology, it is the computer metaphor – the idea that the human being is essentially 'just' a highly complicated processor of information, and that when we have understood fully how that information is processed, we will know all that is necessary about human thought processes.

But analogy is not homology. Just because something can be compared with something else, that doesn't mean that it is the same thing. In some respects, yes, the human brain can be compared with a computer. But in other respects, it operates quite differently. When we move from analogy, which is saying it is 'like' something, to homology, which is saying that it really is the same as that thing, we seriously distort our understanding of what is going on; because from then on we tend to ignore all the differences, and focus only on the similarities.

For many cognitive psychologists, of course, it is overstating the case to say that they see their work as the basis of all psychology. They see their work as part of a more general story – as fitting into the jigsaw, rather than being the whole answer in itself. But if a piece is to fit into a jigsaw, then it must have parts which link in some way with the other pieces, and this is where traditional cognitive psychology falls down. By developing models which are entirely self-contained, without reference to other aspects of human functioning; and by refusing to acknowledge those other dimensions of human life except as a form of 'contamination', traditional cognitive psychology is implicitly arguing that people's thinking is independent of their social, cultural and biological context.

However much lip-service is paid to the jigsaw concept by cognitive psychologists, in the end it is the opportunities offered by the theories which count. If those opportunities preclude integration with other levels of explanation, as they do when other levels are simply seen as optional influences, then the implicit message is that links are unimportant. If the models which cognitive psychologists develop relegate broader aspects of human functioning to one or two input boxes, instead of attempting to integrate them within a coherent model, the message is that those broader aspects are peripheral to human thought. Yet, as we have seen elsewhere, they can be central.

Perhaps the reason why the computer metaphor became so popular with cognitive psychologists is because of its philosophical basis. Using the computer metaphor to 'explain' the brain and how it works is an implicit acceptance of the Cartesian view of 'man as machine', which in our machine-oriented society has become pretty popular with both academics and lay people. I have discussed elsewhere how the mechanistic view of the human being produced by Descartes provided a rationale for treating human beings as 'just' machines during the Industrial Revolution and subsequently, and how it also provides the basis for conventional medical assumptions and for other mechanistic ways of under-standing human behaviour (see Chapter 1).

But the computer metaphor leads to other problems too. Perhaps the most important of these is its intolerance, not just of uncertainty, but also of the more complex forms of reality. Since computers run on principles which derive strictly from formal logic, it is assumed that formal logic is the most important princi-ple that there is. So, for example, human beings who have shown, as they did in the Wason and Johnson-Laird experiments, that their thinking does not accord with formal logic, are assumed to be making 'errors'. The fact that their thinking actually represents something considerably more sophisticated, in that they are apply-ing a complex knowledge of social convention and probability, is considered to be irrelevant. If it isn't strictly logical, it is deemed to be an 'error'.

Many cognitive psychologists have challenged this idea; but the increased adherence to the computer metaphor through the 1980s meant that the work of Gregory, Neisser, Abelson and others, who tried to identify the overarching aspects of cognitive understand-ing, was often ignored. Most modern 'mainstream' cognitive research rests on a fundamental (although unsubstantiated) assumption that cognitive processes are veridical and adhere to the precepts of formal logic. But it isn't as simple as that. As Neisser showed in his comparison of John Dean's memory with the actual events as recorded in the Watergate tapes, someone might get almost every single one of the details wrong, but still get the gist – the social meaning – of what took place completely correct. A cog-nitive psychology which adheres strictly to the computer metaphor is unable to cope with this, because computers don't do that sort of thing.

Of course, some of those working in computer modelling are aware that simple logic is not enough. But the thing which imme-diately strikes a close observer is the naïvety of some of the attempts to rectify this narrowness. For example, I recently attended a paper on computer modelling, in which the researchers had cottoned on to the way that human beings don't just deal with one item of infor-mation at a time. They were very excited about their new 'neural network' system, which allowed the computer to deal with several chains of reasoning at once. Much of the excitement derived from the way that the cross-linkages meant that the logic processes all got jumbled up together and became 'muddy' – their word, not mine.

Just like human thinking, they said! Personally, I don't call applying complex social knowledge 'muddy'; but I suppose that if you live in a world in which things are either correct or errors, then I guess human thinking does look muddy. The dominance of the computer metaphor makes it almost impossible to recognise fundamental qualitative differences between human and computer information processing.

Cognitive psychology and 'objective' science

Another thing that mainstream cognitive psychology and behaviourism have in common is that both are based on the idea that it is possible to refine down what human beings do into some 'pure' form and isolate its essence. For the behaviourists, this was the 'pure' version of learning, the stimulus–response link. For traditional cognitive psychologists, it is the processing of information. Both schools of thought operate on the assumption that identifying the essential nature of these processes will make it possible to work upwards, and to analyse how this essence combines into more complex forms.

But studying human beings by taking some small unit of human behaviour or cognition and studying it in an independent and context-free manner is based on a fallacy – the idea that the behaviour remains essentially the same when it occurs in a real-life context as it is under research conditions. There is any amount of research into the behaviour and understanding of the human subject in the psychological laboratory (for example Silverman, 1977) which shows that people simply don't act in a context-free manner. They are affected by the demand characteristics of the experiment, the relationship with the experimenter and with other subjects, and by their views on the value and social relevance of the study.

Any psychology student encounters this when conducting psychological research of their own – indeed, it's one reason why practical work is such a fundamental part of a psychology degree. But, in accordance with their discipline's socialisation, most psychology students manage to convince themselves that it is their own shortcomings or the limitations of their situation which prevent the 'perfect' experiment. It isn't. The perfect experiment doesn't exist; and nor does the passive research subject who is prepared to do exactly as she is told without even speculating about what the study is for.

What I am saying is that the whole edifice, from Ebbinghaus upwards, is constructed on a myth. It is simply not possible to study human beings in a context-free manner, because however we are trying to study them, we establish some sort of context. And people then behave in ways that they judge appropriate for the context that we have established. Human beings are not like computers. We are social animals, we have biological and affiliative needs, we interact according to complex and sophisticated social rules, and we project the image that we (by and large) wish to project. Even in a psychology experiment.

Moreover, even if we achieved this idea of a 'pure', objective study of human behaviour, what good would it do us? How can human behaviour produced in a 'clinical' setting like a psychology laboratory relate to the real world, which just doesn't operate that way? The very difficulty of establishing 'objective' laboratory conditions should show us how unlike reality those conditions are; and that in itself should tell us something about the value of the evidence about human functioning obtained from such a study. Psychologists who apply cognitive insights in the real world have had considerable success, but that success has always been achieved by compromising on pure 'objectivity' and acknowledging reality, with all its uncontrollable features.

And when we do acknowledge reality, we find that the outcome of our research is often qualitatively different. What about the classic Morris *et al.* (1981) study, in which they found that subjects' memory for word–digit pairs could exceed anything that was previously thought possible?. Normally, if you're asked to remember a set of word–digit pairs based on a single auditory exposure, you wouldn't be likely to do too well. This has been demonstrated so often in the laboratory that it is regarded as a truism – that we only remember 7 ± 2 bits of information at a time. But Morris *et al.* showed that if you are a keen football supporter, and the word–digit pairs that you are hearing are that day's football results, lo and behold, you recall an awful lot more. Hardly surprising, you say? Well, maybe; but what happens then to the limited-capacity theories which have been developed on the basis of 'pure' laboratory work? The simple fact is that we deal with irrelevant information in a way which is qualitatively different from the way we deal with 'real' information. So models developed from how we deal with irrelevant information are, quite simply, not likely to be much use.

In recent years, cognitive psychology has progressed from the nonsense syllable, and it likes to believe that it currently deals much more with 'real' information. And being asked to read a real sentence, or a whole paragraph, is cerstainly much more real than learning a nonsense syllable. But even so, it is about as similar to real reading as the abstract word–digit pair is to the football result. The two are not even likely to utilise the same mechanisms. When you are reading in everyday life your motivation is entirely different (because you are likely to be reading either for your own pleasure, or for some instrumental reason, like studying); the context is different, because each paragraph you read is preceded by something relevant and is going somewhere; the time of day and the setting are different, and so on. It may be better than the nonsense syllable, but it is out of context and still distinctly artificial.

Cognitive psychology and other areas of psychological understanding

That these criticisms reflect a serious deficit in modern cognitive psychology is evidenced by the way in which the insights and theoretical models from cognitive psychology have made very little impact on psychological knowledge in other disciplines.

FIGURE 9.1   Reading is a purposeful activity
Source: Photograph by Steve Redwood.

Its rigid adherence to the computer metaphor renders it inherently useless when it comes to understanding social or developmental cognition, since human beings do not operate like computers. But the developments that have taken place in other disciplines show how strong the need for cognitive insights was.

Social psychology

Increasingly, those cognitive psychologists not enamoured with the computer-oriented aspects of 'cognitive science' have been turning to social cognition as an area in which a socially relevant psychology of cognitive processes is developing. This field operates on entirely different assumptions and with different theoretical models than 'mainstream' cognitive psychology, and, as a consequence, it can deal with 'real life' in a way that information-processing models cannot.

The research area known as social cognition began with the need to explain just how it is that people's understanding of what is going on affects how they act with one another. In part, this has always been an element in social psychology, mainly manifest through research into attitudes. But there is much research which shows that attitudes and behaviour are not always congruent, and it is clear that simply looking at people's attitudes leaves a lot more to be explained.

Social cognition has a number of different areas. One of these is attributional theory – how people explain what is going on, to themselves or to others. Modern attributional theory has the capacity to link together a number of different insights which have arisen in different fields of psychology. For example, we know from the work of Rotter and others that locus of control – perceiving causes as controllable as opposed to uncontrollable – is a crucial factor in stress management. Walking to college on the day of an exam leaves you much less stressed than waiting to see if your lift, or the bus, will turn up; because walking is under your control, whereas the other two options are not.

The study of attributions permeates many aspects of social living. For example, Stratton and Swaffer studied mother's attributions, obtained from hearing them talk about their children while watching them play, and found that mothers who hit their kids saw their children's behaviour as very much less controllable than did mothers of matched control groups. This provided useful pointers for the therapists who were working with these mothers, enabling them to develop an approach which would build up the mothers' sense of agency, and thereby reduce the frustrations which they felt.

This is one specific example of how social cognition has enabled us to investigate areas of day-to-day living in a positive way, by taking the everyday explanations which people make and looking at how these operate. More recently, research into attribution has begun to investigate shared social beliefs – social representations, held by groups of people and taking the form of shared theories about the world and how it works. As an approach, social cognition can handle many more of the levels on which life is lived – coming to terms with the importance of social identification with social and cultural groups rather than simply seeing the individual as an independent information-processor.

There are other forms of social cognition, too. Schank and Abelson's classic work on the unconscious 'scripts' of everyday action which we all follow has enabled us to chart more complex forms of social understanding more closely; and their work has fed back into some of the more socially aware areas of cognitive psychology. In fact, it is a moot point whether Schank and Abelson should be classified in social cognition or in cognitive psychology itself; although if considered as cognitive psychologists, they certainly can't be seen as 'mainstream'.

Developmental psychology

Like social psychology, developmental psychology reached a point at which an understanding of the social cognitive mechanisms developed by the child became essential to further progress. Mainstream cognitive psychology was of no help and therefore, like social psychology, developmental psychology had to develop its own models, entirely independently.

If we look at early research into cognitive development, we find that in orientation it parallels 'mainstream' cognitive psychology, and indeed it achieved its height at a similar time. The highly influential Piagetian model of cognitive development also adopts an individualistic, largely context-free approach to understanding cognition, in which the essential question is how the child comes to terms with solving problems and discrepancy between its prior experience and its immediate sensory input. Essentially, the child is regarded as a context-free problem-solver.

The idea that the social context might be more than simply another factor which the child needs to take into account has been demonstrated by a number of recent studies with children, which have shown how the entire response of the child is dependent on the child's understanding of the social processes which are taking place (see Chapter 8). A changed answer may occur because the same question was repeated, rather than because the child has no stable concept, since repetition of a question from an adult is taken to concur with a social convention meaning that the first answer was wrong. A problem devised using irrelevant settings and objects becomes easy once it is reformulated to a setting with which the child is familiar. And a child exposed to any amount of language through radio and television fails to learn to speak, but makes rapid progress as soon as it has contact with a speaking human being in the form of a speech therapist.

All of these research findings show how the child's social understanding of what is happening is more than simply an added factor, superimposed on some underlying cognitive mechanism. It is a fundamental part of the processes which are going on. Consequently, a very large part of modern research into the psychology of child development is concerned with exploring the child's developing social cognition. For example, Paul Harris's book *Children and Emotion* documents a large chunk of research devoted to exploring the child's theory of mind and their understanding of other people's mental states: research which has given us a lot of insight into why children respond as they do, and which has also led to a greater understanding of the phenomenon of autism.

The models offered by traditional cognitive psychology, or by information-processing models of cognitive development, have been of little value in exploring how children think about other people – and yet, as the previous research has shown, so much of the small child's thought is firmly located within that social context that models based on context-free individualistic problem-solving can account for only a very little of what is going on in the child's mind.

Other areas of psychology
There are other areas of psychology which cognitive psychology has failed to address, despite a clear need for its presence. For example, the fields of advertising and marketing use a number of theoretical models, which tap into some areas of human behaviour and cognition. They draw from several different areas of psychology,

including even Gestalt psychology, but 'mainstream' cognitive psychology is conspicuous by its absence. This is not because the psychologists working in applied psychology are unintelligent or ill-educated; it is because cognitive psychology has little to offer them. It fails to deal with essential human processes.

For example: one of the main motivating factors which advertisers tap into when they are selling products in the modern market-place is that of image projection and impression management. Despite the vast amount of research which has been conducted into imagery, mainstream psychology remains lamentably short of studies investigating the social nuances of different kinds of image, and how these may be manifest in different ways. Yet it is clear from its end product that advertisers have developed highly complex, if largely experiential, concepts about how people use image as part of their understandings of everyday life.

In comparative psychology, too, there are opportunities for some fruitful links which have been entirely overlooked by cognitive psychologists. There has been an increasing amount of research into animal cognition, within both the ethological and the experimental traditions. The ethological tradition, as exemplified by the research of Peter Marler and his colleagues, has thrown up some fascinating work on potential evolutionary precursors of 'words', of preparedness in learning, and, even more interestingly, of natural categories or concepts (Marler, 1982; Gould and Marler, 1987).

When the overall implications of this research are taken into account, what we find is an increasing body of knowledge which could give some very useful insights into the conceptual nature of human thinking. But the involvement of cognitive psychologists in formulating these connections is strikingly non-existent. The same can be said for the research into neurological insights into memory mechanisms (for example Rose, 1992). In both cases, cognitive psychology has the potential for making a solid contribution, but at the time of writing there is no indication that it is doing so.

I would contend, then, that cognitive psychology has sold itself, and the rest of psychology, short. It has failed to provide the alternative which was so badly needed after the dominance of behaviourism. The cognitive obsession with the computer metaphor meant that it fell into the same trap for which it criticised the behaviourists. By defining the human being using a metaphor, and then taking the metaphor as if that were the only possible reality, it rendered itself unable to respond to the real issues and challenges which are being thrown up in other areas of psychology. Where it could have been the linking force between the diversity of psychology's branches, cognitive psychology has gone into a dead-end and become irrelevant to those areas. Despite the efforts of many great cognitive psychologists, the promise of its early years has been lost, and the rest of psychology has had to learn to manage without it.

Chapter 10
Simulating Human Cognition

Despite frequent optimistic pronouncements on the topic, I believe it to be unlikely that it will become possible to simulate human cognitive processes – or at least, not if simulation research continues along the lines which it has been taking. The reason for this is that there are a great many characteristics of human thinking which are well-known to psychologists, yet are commonly ignored by those working in the AI field. They are important, because they represent significant qualitative differences between human and computer systems in the nature of information processing, and unless we are aware of them, we are unlikely to be able to engage in any kind of effective simulation.

Perhaps one of the biggest problems which come up when we are attempting to simulate human cognitive processes is the fact that human beings very rarely respond to the information that they have actually been given. Instead, they respond to the information which they believe that they have been given, and these two types of information are often much less similar than one might expect.

It's really a question of social sophistication. In the early days of computer simulation, much was made of supposed 'errors' in human thinking – occasions where human thinking does not conform to formal logic (for example, Wason and Johnson-Laird, 1972). But when one explores the nature of these errors, it becomes apparent that they are really based on a sophisticated understanding of what is actually likely to be going on.

What I am actually saying is that human beings don't live in a universe governed by formal logic: we live in a world of social probability and judgement, in which the words that people use are not taken literally. Instead, we process human speech in terms of the probable communicative intent of the speaker. And deciphering that probable communicative intent draws on a range of social mechanisms which would be extremely difficult, if not totally impossible, to simulate.

In this chapter we will look briefly at some of the individual processes which challenge the 'naïve logic' view of human thinking, and then go on to look at some of the important group processes which also contribute to the way that human beings think. Some of the individual mechanisms are such that a sophisticated approach might be able to simulate them – given time, research and resources. But the group mechanisms, I believe, are a tougher challenge.

Schemas and personal memory

One aspect of human thinking which presents problems for simplistic approaches to simulation is the more complex aspects of schema formation. Schemas are ways of organising, or representing, information about the world, in such a way as to enable us to plan effective action. They influence what information we are likely to detect, as well as how we are likely to respond to that information. Ulrich Neisser presented (see Figure 10.1) the essence of cognition as a continuous perceptual cycle, in which we pick up information from the environment on the basis of a perceptual search, which in turn is directed by anticipatory schemas. These schemas, in their turn, are modified by the information that we pick up. So while it is possible for us to become aware of unanticipated information, we are much more likely to become aware of it if it is anticipated.

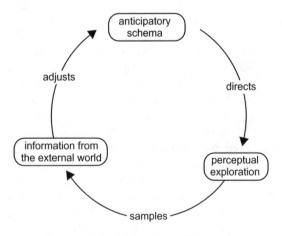

FIGURE 10.1   Neisser's cognitive cycle

That doesn't mean, though, that what we actually perceive or remember will be an exact copy of the information that we were given. As early as 1932, Bartlett showed how we adjust and even distort information, in order to fit it into our personal schemas. As so many researchers have shown, our memory isn't just selective: it also actively changes that which doesn't fit in. In the famous Loftus eye-witness experiments, participants consciously and explicitly remembered details, such as shards of glass, which had simply not been present in the material which they were recalling. The possibility of their presence, however, had been suggested by the vocabulary used to question the participants about the material, and this was enough to generate an explicit and firmly held memory (Loftus and Loftus, 1975).

What this actually means is that the schemas we already hold will exert a considerable influence on the way that we respond to new information. Information which is incongruent is ignored; information which is highly congruent is assimilated; but most information is actively changed, and adopted in a modified or adjusted form. It is that process which channels and directs our actions, and which forms the basis of negotiation for our social representations. And because of this, we often fail to notice information which is not congruent with what we already know.

Social scripts and lay epistemology

Social scripts are special types of schemas which indicate the forms of social action that are likely to occur in a given situation. In a way, scripts are simply an extension of role theory: our understanding of social roles tells us how we should play a particular part, while our awareness of social scripts tells us how the whole scene is likely to develop. Everyday life is full of scripts: from the pre-scripted sequence involved in going to a restaurant to the events that we expect to happen when a couple decide to get married. We are surrounded by social scripts of one form or another: interpersonal scenarios are acted out in song, drama, television, film and newspaper reports, as well as transmitted in individual interaction (Schank and Abelson, 1977).

In other words, social scripts outline possibilities of social action, and provide us with mutually comprehensible ways of conducting our lives. They form an important basis for the sophisticated social judgement which we use in problem-solving. Yet people do, at times, act in ways which are contrary to social scripts – our behaviour is not fully determined by them. What this implies is that an attempt at simulation to any complex degree would also need to take account of the way that scripts shape our probability judgements.

People do other things which could not be predicted by naïve logical models of human thinking. One of the most interesting mechanisms uncovered by researchers into lay epistemology is the mechanism known as 'freezing', in which people will cling to, or revert back to, established beliefs even in the face of directly contradictory information. As a general rule, we don't explore alternative hypotheses: we go for the most likely explanation and stick to that. And even for unusual events, according to Kruglanski (1980), we generally only develop one or two ideas, and then fix on one particular hypothesis as an explanation.

For example: in one study research participants were asked to rate a series of suicide notes in terms of whether they were likely to be genuine or not. The participants were then given false information about how accurate they had been. Even after the researchers had admitted lying, and revealed the evidence, the participants continued to believe what they had originally been told – they had taken no notice of the new information at all.

The motivation underpinning this process is thought to derive from three factors. The first is a need for structure – we have to organise what we know in such a way as to give us clear guidance for action. The second is to do with what we wish to believe. People have their own personal values, ideas and images of themselves; and will tend to select those beliefs which fit them. And the third is to do with our need for validity. As a general rule, we don't believe things if we know that they are not true; but sometimes it doesn't really matter that much whether they are true or not.

This last point may need a bit of explaining. For example: if we know someone only very slightly, it doesn't really matter much to us whether they are clean in their personal habits. So we might generally accept, or freeze on to, a belief that they are OK, even though we see them looking a bit scruffy from time to time. In this example, we have a low need for validity, and so we can cope with a bit of inconsistency between what we observe and what we believe. But if we were about to share a flat with that person, the need for validity regarding that particular belief would become much more important, in that someone who is scruffy might also turn out to be untidy, lazy and so on. So in that case, our high need for validity would unfreeze the belief, and we would be open to a number of different possibilities. A high need for validity gives us the motivation to keep our belief options open and to gather more information.

These, then, are a few of the individual mechanisms which operate in human thinking, and render it a great deal more sophisticated than we might initially suspect. But there are other aspects to human cognition, too, which are even more complex to deal with.

Social identification

One of these is the process of social identification. It is fundamental to human thinking to classify the social world in terms of 'them-and-us' groups (Tajfel and Turner, 1979). The origins of this conceptual mechanism lie deep in our evolutionary past as social animals, and the mechanism exerts an overriding influence on the way that we receive and process information. That influence is so great that we can entirely dismiss information coming from one source while totally accepting the same information coming from a different one. If it comes from 'one of us', we can see it as valid, important and relevant; but if it comes from 'one of them', we may see it as unimportant, invalid and insignificant.

Moreover, we all have many social identifications, and we can switch from one to another during the course of a single conversation, if such a switch becomes salient. A domestic argument about who does the washing-up can transform in an instant from a personal discussion into an intergroup conflict, where each participant is acting as the representative of their gender group. This transformation results in incoming information being processed entirely differently, and with reference to an extensive range of prior knowledge, schemas and assumptions (Hogg and Abrams, 1988).

Social groups also differ systematically in power and status, and so belonging to a particular group has a direct effect on our own self-esteem. This has implications for how, and whether, a listener will process information. People make attributions about the credibility of information which they receive, on the basis of their assumptions about the vested or predicted interests of particular groups. But – and this is another problem inherent in social identification – this is not an either/or situation. Intergroup conflict is not inevitable, and people can often interact positively with members of different groups. When they do so, their schemas and assumptions are still in force, but may result in information being accepted more rather than less readily. When it comes to illness, for instance, we may accept the word of a doctor more readily than the word of one of our own family.

Personal constructs and social representations

Another very basic feature of human thinking is our tendency to disregard our direct experience in favour of both personal constructs and social representations of reality. Personal constructs are the individual theories which we form on the basis of our personal experience, and which we use to make sense of the world around us (Kelly, 1955). Each person has their own unique construct pattern, and this acts as a kind of filter, which can result in widely varying individual responses to the same information. This in itself represents a major challenge to simulations based on models of human thought which assume that it is based on straightforward or naïve logic. But personal constructs are developed on the basis of personal experience, and so may be amenable to simulation, in more complex systems.

What is more difficult to simulate, however, are the social representations which we also use in everyday cognition. Social representations are at the interface between ideology and individual cognition. They are shared beliefs, world-views and assumptions held by particular groups in society. The French psychologist Serge Moscovici described how social representations consist of a central nucleus, which is ideological or functional in nature for the group which holds it, and tends to remain pretty consistent. But they also have peripheral elements which are negotiated by the individual through conversation and other inputs, and are therefore more variable. The central core links with deeply-rooted cultural and philosophical perspectives to do with perceptions of human nature and the world, while the peripheral elements link with personal constructs, schemas and personal awareness.

Like personal constructs, social representations act to determine individual responses to information. But they are firmly rooted in social identity processes, and in the person's culturally-centred world-view. They are also directly functional for the individual, providing explanations and theories for why the world is like it is. This makes them much less malleable than personal constructs, which can be disconfirmed by personal experience. People will hold to social representations even in the face of directly disconfirming experiences, and in situations where they would re-evaluate or revise a personal construct.

There are problems of scale associated with both social identification and social representations. Social representations encapsulate complex historical, cultural and ideological knowledge, and can operate at levels ranging from familial to cross-cultural. Social groups can be large-scale, such as gender, nationality or language-speaking cultures; yet they can also be small-scale, represented by family, employment or residential district. Long-term group identification and social representations are closely interlinked, and apparently contradictory social representations can be held concurrently by the same individual, where they relate to different social identities. Yet both social identifications and social representations will determine how a particular person will process information.

Over all, then, what we have in human cognition is a whole complex of different mechanisms, both individual and social, which shape and sometimes even determine the cognitions which we experience. The processing of incoming information is far from being the straight-line procedure that it is in many computer models, and it isn't simply the product of lots of different straight-line mechanisms either. There is absolutely no guarantee, when it comes to human cognition, that the outcome will reflect the input. All of which means that I personally doubt whether it will ever become possible to simulate these processes effectively. What is certain is that doing so would require a very different approach from the ones which are being adopted at the moment.

Chapter 11

Eco-psychology

As a new awareness of ecology and of ecological balance begins to penetrate our consumer consciousness, where is psychology? Is there a case for a new approach to psychology – an eco-psychology, dedicated to exploring the relationship between the human being and its ecological environment? This chapter aims to raise that question, and to explore some of the ways that psychology has been moving towards such an approach. It is my private belief that psychology has, or could have, a great deal to offer in the context of this new awareness of the importance of our environment. But much of what it has to offer is scattered across the discipline. Whether these disparate threads can be woven into a viable garment remains to be seen.

The mind in context

Certainly, the word ecology has permeated the psychological vocabulary in recent years. Ecological validity has been a central issue in much cognitive and social research recently, and the trend shows no sign of abating. Not very long ago, laboratory-bound methodologies seriously limited how far psychology could penetrate into everyday living; but times have been a-changing. Psychology has developed a range of new conceptual and methodological tools, and now shows every sign of really becoming able to handle everyday experience.

Cognitive psychology, for example, has become increasingly sophisticated in its awareness of and its ability to deal with cognition in everyday living (for example, Neisser, 1982; Smyth *et al.*, 1987) – or, at least, some cognitive psychology has, as we have seen in the past couple of chapters. Indeed, apart from the issue of ecological validity, the other major use of the word 'ecological' which emerges in psychological vocabulary occurs in the context of J. J. Gibson's radical theory of perception, in which he approached perception, not as dispassionate computer-style information processing, but in terms of its evolutionary function: what a living organism needs to know in order to be able to act effectively in the real world. Although much of the research into Gibson's theory has operated within conventional laboratory paradigms, the conceptual shift is still there. Both people and animals have evolved to operate in the real world, and their cognitive mechanisms reflect that.

Neisser's theory of cognition, which was perhaps most clearly expressed in 1976, is very firmly located in the real world, rather than in an idealised computer metaphor. Neisser argued that it is our continual interaction with the world, and the continual modification of our expectations and search procedures as a result, which form the basis of all cognition, not just perception. The model argues, strongly, that to separate cognition from the world in which it takes place is unrealistic: that simply isn't how it works. We are continually interacting, cognitively as well as physically, with our environment. Both of these theoretical approaches are quite different from the idea that as human beings we stand somehow distant from what is around us, appraising and processing the information we receive in a detached, impartial way.

In the social arena, ever since Rom Harré showed how an ethogenic methodology could capture the everyday meanings of social interaction (for example, Harré 1979; March, Rosser and Harré, 1978), the discipline has been opening up to new areas. Even our close relationships are becoming more susceptible to psychological investigation (Duck, 1988; Sternberg, 1987). We have developed social psychological theories which can deal with the way that people interact as members of social groups which differ in power and status. And we have an increasingly well-developed knowledge about the processes and mechanisms of social representations – how people and groups explain what is going on in the world around them. In short, social psychology is well on the way to dealing with those complex areas of human experience that used to be avoided because they couldn't be studied very easily in the laboratory. So what about the human relationship with the natural world?

Ecological activists argue that our whole relationship with, and attitude towards, our environment needs to be rethought. We need to see ourselves are part of the world – as participating in it – rather than as independent of it. The traditional Western stance towards the world has been of the world as separate, and distant, from the individual. It is not a perception which was shared by the great ecologically sensitive non-technological cultures, such as those of the Native Americans, whose careful management of their environment produced a land which was virtually overflowing with wildlife. It is the Western attitude of separation, many ecologists believe, which has led to the exploitation of nature and the disregard for natural balance, the results of which we see so clearly today.

Empiricism and self-perception

We can trace the development of this attitude in Western philosophical thought. In the early chapters of this book, we explored some of the implications of Cartesian dualism, and this too has been a factor. But other empiricist philosophers were involved as well. For instance: Locke, Berkeley and Hume all took as their starting point the idea that human beings have five senses: sight, hearing, touch, smell and taste. Their ideas about the nature of knowing and the individual's relationship with the world were entirely predicated on that basis. Yet we now know, from both physiological and psychological evidence, as well as our own experience, that we have more senses than that. We have at least four internal senses as well, which tell us about the internal state of the body, movements of the muscles and joints, and so on. And if we take these senses into account as well, when we are looking at how people receive information about the world, we end up with a very different model.

What essentially happens is that we lose the idea that our senses somehow present us with a distant, detached, image of the world. Instead, they give us an image of the world and ourselves as we are located in it. External experience becomes linked with internal experience. We connect how we, personally, feel with what we are perceiving through our 'external' senses. At its most extreme, this recognition challenges the idea that we can somehow operate on the external world and remain unchanged ourselves – the basis of much ecological activism. At the very least, it opens up ways that we can link our internal feelings with external situations.

The concept has interesting implications, not least in terms of our relationship with, and perceptions of, the world. For example, how much have we studied the relationship between minor illness and perception of the world? As an extreme hayfever sufferer, I (and, regrettably, those close to me) have become aware of how strongly the condition affects my emotions. When I'm fighting a hayfever attack I become irritable and intolerant, which as a general rule is not all that characteristic. From talking to other sufferers and their families I have found that others, too, experience similar mood/attitude changes. Colds and flu seem to affect some people in similar ways. Have we more than just anecdotal data about the relationship between health and emotion?

The Ifaluk of Micronesia recognise these issues. In their language, they have five different words for anger (Lutz, 1990). One word, *tipmochmoch*, is used to describe the feeling of irritability which is often experienced by people who are ill. This is seen as being quite different from the irritability which occurs when relatives have not fulfilled their obligations (*nguch*), the kind of anger which arises from frustration or helplessness in the face of personal misfortunes or some other unfairness (*tang*), the anger which builds up gradually when a whole series of little unpleasant events occur (*lingeringer*), or the sense of 'justifiable anger' or righteous indignation which occurs in the face of moral unfairness or injustice (*song*).

If it comes to that, exploring how human beings really do relate to their worlds also raises questions about the psychological effects of degrees of physical fitness? Why does the world seem so much more pleasant when we are fit and well? Why is it easier to be optimistic when we have had a good meal or a good night's sleep? Cartesian, machine-like metaphors of the human body simply can't begin to get close to explaining these psychological phenomena, but they are too widely known in lay experience for us to ignore or dismiss them totally. If we can explain 'jogger's euphoria' in terms of endorphins and enkephalins, can we go any further than that? We've known about psychosomatic illness for over a hundred years now, so what about the psychology of normal health? What do we know about influences of the body on the mind, or feedback loops between bodily state and psychological well-being? Does this connect with the phenomenon of state-dependent learning? Eco-psychology is concerned with gathering up the disparate bits of knowledge in this area, and attempting to integrate them into a whole body of knowledge.

The physical environment

And then there's the question of the interaction between our physical states and the physical environment that we are in. For example, one phenomenon which has always struck me as meriting far more attention than psychologists have given it is our reactions to being in 'natural' places. Going for walks in the country, sitting by the sea, gazing at a waterfall: these are all powerfully evocative images. Why? What is it that they evoke?

Whatever it is, it is powerful enough for us to recognise it instantly. Argyle and Crossland (1987) used phrases like this to evoke positive emotions in their research participants, and found that people had no difficulty relating to the emotion itself. When they analysed descriptions of these and many other emotions, they found that they were particularly strong on 'potency' and 'spiritual' dimensions. That's something which could usefully be explored by an eco-psychologist. But the simple fact that their research participants could immediately relate to this type of description on a personal level, and recall their own associated emotional experiences with such clarity and consistency, is a message in itself.

Anecdotally, many people are aware of how much a walk in the country, or by the seashore, can affect their emotions. Feelings of relaxation and tranquillity from a visit to some remote beauty spot or the sense of 'refreshment of the spirit' so often described in novels and other literature seem to be common in many people's experience. Carl Jung was brave enough to attempt to tackle this on a theoretical level, but not many psychologists have looked at it since. On the other hand, psychoanalytical methodology was more suited for expressing such interests, certainly by comparison with the more rigid, behaviouristically influenced methodologies which dominated traditional psychology for so long. But psychological methodology has come a long way since the 1970s, and we are far more able to encompass broad perspectives now.

Hay and Morisey (1978) showed that, according to surveys, about a third of the population report having experienced religious-style mystical experiences. I don't know whether this is related to the above issue or not; but I would think it worth investigating. My guess would be that if people were similarly asked about the sometimes quite overwhelming semi-mystical emotions often associated with being in outstandingly beautiful natural environments, the figure would be far higher. There may be a qualitative difference between the two types of experience, or the difference may only be a matter of intensity. But anything that occurs so frequently should be a matter for psychological investigation.

There have been a few attempts to chart semi-mystical experiences. For example, Benewick and Holton (1987) interviewed members of the crowd during a large open-air Mass held during the Pope's visit to Britain, and afterwards. People described it as one of the most deeply moving, spiritual experiences of their lives. Not least in this experience was the sense of sharing brought about by being a member of such a large, peaceful crowd, and knowing that for others, too, it was a deeply meaningful experience.

On a more mundane level, there are also supposed psychologically positive effects from simply spending a lot of time in the open air. On a personal level – that is, anecdotally – I know that a day spent outdoors always seems to leave me feeling relaxed and contented (unless it's the hayfever season). Gardening, fishing and walking are the three most popular recreational activities in this country (with the exception of watching TV): I don't think this is accidental. Afficionados of each talk of the psychological benefits of the time that they spend outdoors as self-evident. Do psychologists know about these psychological benefits? Are we, at least, looking into them? I hope so.

The trouble is, though, that all of this is really only anecdotal evidence. And anecdotal evidence isn't good enough. So eco-psychology needs to engage in systematic research to find out whether there is any real psychological validity underlying these common everyday ideas, or whether they are all simply a wide-spread delusion – like the illusion of veridical memory, or the social delusion that people will stand up and confront authority rather than obeying an order which goes against conscience. In both these cases, psychological research has shown that, just because something is a commonplace belief, it doesn't mean that it is true. But in other cases, psychological research has found that everyday beliefs are well-grounded. Without research, we can't tell which is which.

Vicky Rippere (1988) and others (for example, Rippere and Adams, 1982) have been at pains to point out the importance of clinical ecology for clinical psychology. Food allergies may seem a far cry from the effects of global warming or the destruction of the ozone layer, and if we stick to a rigidly dualistic interpretation of behavioural change and food allergy, then clinical ecology may be seen as having little to offer a wider perspective. However, as Edwards and Owens (1984) point out, clinical ecology has its holistic implications too, and could be construed as carrying some direct implications about the interaction between the human psyche and its environment. There is potential here for much further exploration, and not just into the effects of foodstuffs.

Social contacts

And then there's our relationship with animals. Keeping pets, as far as I can tell, seems to be an activity in which human beings all over the globe engage. Sociobiologists emphasise the importance of looking at 'universals' of human behaviour: does this tell us anything? It also seems to be fairly well-established that ownership of the right type of pets can significantly reduce the risk of heart disease. The main theoretical explanation that I have heard argues in terms of the importance of tactile contact and stroking in reducing tension and stress, but there may be other explanations. This too strikes me as being the type of question that eco-psychology needs to explore; and there is some sign that psychologists are beginning to do so. A recent article in the *British Journal of Psychology*, for example, looked at the social aspects of dog-walking, in terms of interactions with other people, and the increased likelihood of small social greetings occurring during the process (McNicholas and Collis, 2000). It's a start.

There are questions, too, about the location of the human being in their community. Disparate items of information suggest how important the mechanisms of cooperation, reconciliation and social awareness are to people. Studies of the self-concept show how the idea of the self as an independent entity, away from its social network, appears to be a peculiarly Western phenomenon – and isn't even all that valid in the West, since self-concept has been repeatedly shown to be so dependent on social factors. And again, there are social phenomena which need to be explained. For example, why is it that, with such *overwhelming* societal propaganda warning us away from being friendly with strangers, people are still willing to help one another out?

De Waal (1989) showed how reconciliation is an almost completely under-researched area. We know a great deal about the propagation and maintenance of aggression, but almost nothing about the mechanisms of reconciliation. Yet, when you think about it, reconciliation is the social glue which holds everything together. Without the ability to resolve aggressive interactions, no social community – animal or human – could remain whole. It would simply fly apart. If we are truly to look at the human being in an ecological context, that has to include the social context as well. We have evolved as social animals (more about that in Chapter 14), and that means that the social aspects of our environment are just as important as the physical ones.

Rom Harré proposed that one of the most useful ways that we could explore social living was to begin to look at social life, not in terms of discrete acts or single interactions, but in terms of meaningful episodes. By taking the episode as the unit of analysis, we would be able to apply some of the analytical tools which allow us to look at what is happening in a social situation – our knowledge of social scripts, roles, non-verbal communication and so on – and piece them all together in terms of their human meaning. Such an approach to understanding social living would be much more able to incorporate the ecological influences of context and setting than the traditional approach of studying social acts in isolation.

Ecological activism

There are other, more obvious topics for eco-psychology, too. One is the whole question of ecological activism. There are questions about which individuals are more or less likely to become ecologically concerned, and also about which people are more or less susceptible to changing their lifestyles. Is it age-related? Does it make a noticeable difference if we teach children about it in school? Did the 'sixties' have anything to do with it – did its simplistic philosophies lay the groundwork for an appreciation of ecological concerns in later life? Or is it primarily a response from a younger generation, intolerant of the material values and/or naïve romanticism of their elders.

Since the 1980s, lead-free petrol has become the norm; recycling (of some products, at least) has become better integrated into everyday living; and consumer demand for organic foods has skyrocketed. But on the other hand, dependence on the car has increased dramatically, and traffic density is higher than ever. We also need to understand the attitude and attributional changes which underlie the whole process. How do people partition up ecologically sensitive behaviours, in cognitive terms? How does the increasing recognition of the ecological damage from cars map on to increased use of cars as the mode of transport? Is there cognitive dissonance, or are these seen as entirely unrelated?

This raises questions about the motivations for lifestyle change, too. Do people who aim for lifestyle change seeing themselves differently, in relation to the world? Does that relate to their self-efficacy beliefs, or to locus of control? And what about the behavioural patterns of lifestyle change? How do those who are intellectually committed go about changing their lifestyles? Are there sudden discontinuities, 'stages' in ecological awareness, or a continuous, gradual adaptation? Do people sustain their efforts once they begin, and what causes them to 'give up', if they do?

This leads us inevitably into the area of social representations – the ideologically-based shared beliefs about the nature of the world and the human being that we all hold. We need to explore how people understand ecological issues. My own research into this area shows that public awareness is very diverse, and that there is a tremendous amount of straightforward factual confusion – despite the vast amount of public education in the area. There is much more to integrating awareness of ecological issues in the public mind than simply expressing the facts clearly.

There's the motivational side of things, too. We know from clinical psychology how devastating the effects of learned helplessness can be, and how important it is to the human being to have manageable goals and a sense of agency. But global ecological issues, as a general rule, carry their own pessimistic message of gloom and futility. So what does our existing psychological knowledge about human motivation have to tell us about getting ecological messages across?

Alternative epistemologies

These are some of the more apparent avenues which an eco-psychology might explore. It's not a definitive list: there are many other possibilities. Some of the questions which could be raised might be too far 'on the fringe' for many of us, but might still provide useful insights. For instance, what about animism? If we take a cross-cultural perspective, and include our own everyday experience (rather than the 'official' view of what Westerners believe), we find that animism is endemic in human thought patterns – whether it be in talking to one's computer, ascribing malevolent intent to a car that breaks down on a particularly crucial morning, apologising to a tree before one cuts it down, or locating the spirits of one's ancestors in a sacred rock face. Why is it so widespread? Could animism perhaps be seen as a manifestation of a basic tendency to see oneself as part of and taking part in the world, rather than as a entity separate and distinct from the rest of the natural world – an 'individual'?

It has long been a truism that non-technological cultures may have a great deal to teach us about living with our planet. But if it is going to tell us anything, then we have to be ready to listen: we need to look, seriously, at the concepts in non-technological cultures, and ask what they can tell us. I am reminded of a paper by Horton (1967) on traditional African approaches to medicine. Typically, if someone falls sick from an infectious disease, a traditional medicine practitioner will look for social stress as a source: has the patient had any recent disagreements with friends or neighbours? That could be the spell which produced the sickness.

To Western ears, this makes no sense: we believe that we know how infectious diseases are transmitted. But Horton pointed out that in a country with a high infant mortality rate, those who survive to adulthood are, almost by definition, those with a high natural immunity to such diseases. In such cases, the question is why they became susceptible – why their natural resistance was lowered – and in that context, given how stress suppresses immune functioning, looking for social stressors with a view to resolving them makes a great deal of sense. The question is whether one sees the human being within the context of its ecosystem or separate from it. Failing to appreciate the relationship can produce an inadequate, or even distorted, understanding of what is going on and why.

The ecological movement argues that we all have to change our consciousness if we are going to come to terms with living on this planet. Psychology should be at the forefront of that change. Our discipline has a tradition of considering how human beings are affected by their environment, but has usually only considered small, discrete bits of that influence, so out of context as to be of only limited value. But recent developments in environmental psychology have broadened our perspectives in that direction, and the recent broadening of psychological methodology gives us the conceptual and analytical tools to look at less tangible aspects of human experience. So isn't it time that we took a further step and began to explore, systematically, just what an eco-psychology might have to offer us, in our attempt to understand the human being?

Chapter 12

The Politics of Nature and Nurture

One of the first questions in psychology that a new student learns about is the nature-nurture debate. A nature-nurture debate is concerned with what causes something to develop. On one side are the nativists, who see development as arising from innate factors – from genetic inheritance. On the other side are the empiricists, who see development as occurring because of experience and learning. Nature-nurture debates are often presented as being simply academic disputes; but they are actually much more than that. They form the basis of the way that we organise our society, and also of our attitudes towards one another. And as such, they are highly political issues.

The philosophical background

Nature-nurture debates have a long philosophical history, stemming from three seventeenth-century European philosophers: Thomas Hobbes, René Descartes and John Locke. Their ideas contain two interconnected issues, each of which has been influential in psychological thinking. The first is biological determinism – how far the human being is determined by its animal nature. The other is whether human mental capacities are innate – inherited through genetic transmission – or whether they arise through experience.

Hobbes was one of the first biological reductionists. He argued that human beings were simply the product of their biological natures; and that as a result of this, human relationships in the 'natural' state were typified by competition, threat and fear, and the wish to achieve recognition or glory. So, Hobbes argued, organised society had to be constructed in such a way as to minimise the damage done by 'human nature'. Left to themselves,

Hobbes believed, people would engage in all-out warfare, so society needed to keep its members in check.

This view of human nature is still common today. The idea that people need to be controlled 'for their own good' is one which is a fundamental principle of modern social organization. While we see it to some extent in any organised society, it appears in its most extreme form in totalitarian countries. Biological determinism is an important belief for these societies. It justifies repressive social practices by maintaining that people's own natures are their own worst enemies: that aggression is innate and unavoidable, and that rigid social control leads to the greatest happiness of the greatest number. As a result, it was a common argument in, for instance, Stalinist Russia and Maoist China, as well as other totalitarian states.

As a form of argument, biological determinism is still very widespread. It receives a great deal of media coverage, through popularisers such as Desmond Morris and Richard Dawkins. If we look carefully at their ideas, which we will be doing in the next chapter, we find that they propound the view that people's tendencies to socially destructive behaviours are biological and inevitable, and cannot be helped. This is a form of argument which has descended directly from Hobbes. And it is intimately linked with the nature/nurture question, because it rests entirely on an assumption that people's natures are inherited.

By contrast, Descartes argued that the human mind is a completely separate entity from the body. The body, in Descartes's view, is purely a machine, operating like a machine and not influencing the mind at all. The mind, on the other hand, is the seat of reason and the essence of being human – hence Descartes's famous definition of what it is to be human: 'I think, therefore I am'. This dualism of Descartes did not ignore 'animal nature' in human beings, but held that it was the base state, which could be overcome by reason and rationality. As such, Cartesian philosophy presented a different picture to that of Hobbes, and one which was very appealing to the emerging rationalistic/materialistic society of the time – a society which was just breaking free from the theological domination of the Middle Ages.

However, with the later development of evolutionary theory, the mind–body distinction which Descartes made was challenged. Evolutionists argued that there was no qualitative difference between human beings and other animals – an argument which opened the way for Cartesian views to be linked with biological reductionism.

Essentially, the link happened through the connection with nativism. Descartes was strongly of the belief that human mental faculties were innate, and not changeable. His nativist perspective on mental ability has dominated European philosophical and psychological thinking to the present day.

The other side of the nature-nurture debate came from a line of thinking which was perhaps most clearly expressed by the philosopher John Locke (1632–1704). He was one of the early empiricists, who considered that all human knowledge comes ultimately from experience. As such, it was acquired through the senses: vision, hearing, touch, taste and smell. Locke envisaged the mind of the human infant at birth as a *tabula rasa* – a blank slate on which the child's experiences would be written. Meaningful thought and ideas emerged from the association of different sensory experiences, allowing the child to identify regularities and patterns.

Locke's thinking was extremely influential in many areas of human society, including the political sphere. It has always, for instance, been a major underlying philosophical assumption on the part of social reformers, because it carries the crucial implication that human nature isn't fixed and determined, but can be moulded and developed through experience. It formed a philosophical basis for the revolutionary movements of the eighteenth century as well as those of later times, influencing revolutionaries such as Thomas Paine, whose ideas were so fundamental to the newly formed United States of America. It also formed a philosophical basis for the massive social engineering projects of Soviet Russia, and their attempts to create the New Soviet Man through social education and social restructuring.

For people who were trying to found a new society not dominated by the feudal and religious oppression of the old Europe, Locke's ideas were a breath of fresh air. By suggesting that human nature was essentially learned, Locke had implied that new forms of social interaction and social structures were possible: that the old order was not inevitable. In later times, as we have seen, Locke's associationism also provided the basis for the emergence of the behaviourist school of thought in psychology – which, in its day, was also radical, even though it may seem rather repressive to modern eyes.

So much for the philosophical background. It's important, though, for us to recognise that the various perspectives put forward in these debates represent forms of thinking which are not recent and modern, but have permeated society for hundreds of years. During their long history, they have appeared in many different forms, and have fuelled massive political and social change. So perhaps it's understandable that people get a bit heated about them.

Nature and nurture in psychological theory

There are many nature-nurture debates in psychological theory, and, as I shall show, some of them have at times carried social implications which were literally a matter of life and death. Through the twentieth century, there was a steady nature-nurture debate raging in society, with views ranging from extreme nativism to extreme empiricism. Nativist ideas remain the dominant perspective in our society, and their popularity can be seen in the amount of publicity given to those who propound it. The work of Desmond Morris, for instance, receives massive media acclaim; as do Richard Dawkins's ideas about the 'selfish gene'. Alternative, non-nativist ideas such as those put forward by Steven Rose or Stephen Jay Gould receive little publicity.

Incidentally, it is worth noting here that modern psychologists see human development rather differently. Instead of seeing it as a straight either-or question, modern psychologists perceive a continuous interaction between the two. Biological predispositions may guide development in certain directions, but how that development proceeds depends entirely on our experience with the environment. We call this a *dialectical* relationship between inheritance and the environment. They each contribute to the whole, and are completely interconnected, not competing, alternatives. We will come back to this idea later.

The animal language debate

Many of the nature-nurture debates which a psychology student encounters appear to be relatively innocuous. It is difficult, really, to get excited about the political implications of the nature-nurture debates on perception or language – if, indeed, there are any. But when we look at the evidence for these debates too, they show in the end that there is an interaction between biological predispositions and the environment; and that social experience is an important part of it. In addition, one particular feature of the nature-nurture debate on language highlights an interesting issue.

For the hereditarians, the idea that chimpanzees might be able to learn human language is anathema. Language above all else must be seen as innate for humans and no other species. So attempts to teach animals human languages were actually quite threatening, and resulted in a complicated game of 'moving the goalposts', such that whatever any chimpanzee achieved was described as not 'really' language. Each time a new achievement was reached, the criteria for what 'real' language was were adjusted, to make sure that it didn't really count.

The chimpanzee Lana, for example, was deemed to be not using language because she did not communicate spontaneously with her keepers. But Washoe and the other Oklahoma chimps did communicate spontaneously, so all of a sudden the most important issue was whether their requests used the correct word-order. The fact that this wasn't even a criterion which could be applied universally to human languages were totally ignored. By the time the whole research programme was torpedoed by Terrace in the early 1980s (on inaccurate grounds), the criteria for what counted as 'real' language had got to the point where it was questionable whether a typical toddler's speech, matched to those criteria, would have been seen as language either.

The point about this was that throughout this whole research programme, the arguments of the critics came not from informed scientific judgement but from predetermined views. Criteria were manipulated simply to make sure that the same criticisms could be maintained. Whether one believes that what these chimpanzees did was truly language or not, a 'scientific' approach should surely involve applying consistent standards, rather than moving the goalposts in mid-debate.

Opposition to social change

Nativist arguments have more significant uses too. They have consistently been used to argue against social change, even on a relatively trivial level. Take the case of dyslexia, for instance. It has been argued – see, for instance, Whittaker (1982) – that since its original inception, the concept of dyslexia has become so broad that it is now applied to almost any difficulty in spelling which the child encounters. And this has served to distract attention from poor teaching and low expectations on the part of teachers.

I, personally, would not dispute that a specific disorder known as dyslexia exists. Nor would I dispute that for those who have it, it can produce real difficulties. But I would seriously question whether three-quarters of those children who are deemed to be 'dyslexic' really have the disorder, and I would also question the role which the concept has come to play in society. Too often, it has been used for teachers (or parents) to avoid taking responsibility for failure when a particular child doesn't enjoy the kind of learning which school provides, and so doesn't learn to read particularly quickly. The idea of an inherited disorder distracts attention from more serious social questions, such as the quality of teaching or parental expectation, and so avoids identifying a need for social change.

In fact, nativist ideas dominate education, at least in Britain. The firm belief in a child's 'ability' has resulted in millions of children being deprived of access to higher levels of education – and, increasingly, condemned to a life on the dole, as opportunities for unskilled workers die away. Interestingly, this doesn't apply in other countries. Both American and Russian educational systems are based on the premise that children are all educable, and some 60 per cent of the population of the United States go on to some form of higher education. The British proportion is only a fraction of this.

The difference can be seen perhaps most clearly in the role which testing plays in the educational systems of England and America. In the United States, children are tested frequently, and all are expected to achieve the specified level of attainment for their year group. Should a child fail a test, this is taken as an indication that it needs to go through that part of the curriculum another time, perhaps with extra help, so that it won't fail it next time. So tests are used diagnostically, to help the child to progress.

In England, on the other hand, testing has always been used to exclude people from education. Major examinations like the 11+, GCE and CSE or in modern times GCSE exams, A levels and degree examinations have all acted as a filter, weeding out the 'weaker' candidates. The test result is taken as an indication that the child isn't capable of such learning, not that it simply needs to go over the material again.

It's also interesting to note which aspects of psychological theory are accepted in the UK's education system. Piaget, for instance, regarded the concept of 'biological readiness' and the developmental stages to be very minor parts of his theory. What mattered, in his view, was the child's interaction with its environment. But it was the concept of readiness which was adopted wholesale by teachers and teacher trainers, with its implicit message that there was no point trying to teach children things before they were biologically capable of it. Some educationalists, such as Shayer and Adey, even argued that some children would never become capable of formal operations – for genetic reasons.

Of course, the private sector in education in Britain didn't adopt Piagetian theory in quite such a wholesale manner. They continued to teach 5-year-olds measurement and calculations, and to push children into achieving educational success. As a result, the gap between the private and public sectors of education became even wider – and with it, the gap in educational expectations for working- and middle-class children.

Recent theories of socio-cognitive development have shown how important the human factor is in what children can learn: Donaldson, for instance, showed how children have no problem with Piagetian tasks if they are placed in a human context. It is only when the tasks are decontextualised, or abstract, that the children have difficulties. 'Decentring' was no problem when the child had to hide a boy doll from a policeman doll; but was a problem when the child was asked to look at photographs of mountains that didn't have any social meaning. So in theories of cognitive development, too, we have a hidden nature-nurture debate, with significant social implications.

The evidence for nativist ideas

But when we look at the evidence for nativist theories, time and again we find it to be highly questionable. For example: one of the most famous psychological studies of inherited character appeared in psychological textbooks in the first part of the twentieth century, and purported to be a study of a family known as the Kallikaks. These people were portrayed as hard-core moral degenerates, who enjoyed living in the gutter and who could not be reformed, because their propensities were inherited. The textbook accounts were accompanied by photographs of members of the family, showing them as evil and ferocious in facial appearance – although a photograph of a female member of the family kept in an institution showed her looking serene and pleasant. Gould (1981) pointed out that the photographs of the 'unpleasant' members of the family were clearly altered, to make them appear more ferocious: this was done so clumsily that any modern child could perceive it.

Although it may seem to be a trivial example, the doctoring of the photographs raises some significant points. Mainly, it highlights how evidence for the debate has been overstated, distorted, or even entirely fabricated. Which in turn raises the question: why? Why is it that purveyors of a supposedly scientific theory feel the need to distort their evidence in this way? The answer, of course, lies in the political nature of the theory. The case of the Kallikaks was used as a political tool to demonstrate the futility of trying to improve the lot of the poorer people in society: their economic degeneration simply reflected their innate characters, and as such there was nothing society could do to improve them. Instead, the nativists argued, they should be put into institutions, and sterilised to ensure that they did not pass on their unsavoury genes to another generation.

Dubious scientific practice is not uncommon in the hereditarian position. Take, for instance, the idea that schizophrenia is inherited. This is almost an article of faith with many members of the medical profession, and even a few psychologists, although not all that many. It is often asserted to have been thoroughly proven in the past, by twin studies. It also goes hand in hand with the idea of schizophrenia being caused by brain chemicals: the idea is that an inherited gene stimulates the production, or overproduction, of whatever brain chemical is fashionable at the time, and this causes the schizophrenia. Various chemicals have been proposed to fit this role at different times: the dopamine hypothesis of schizophrenia, put forward in 1972, was one of the first, but many others have also been proposed, such as acetylcholine or gamma-amino-butyric acid.

But when we actually scrutinise the evidence, we find that it all goes back to a set of twin studies performed by Kallman in 1938. This is regarded as a classic study, and is quoted uncritically in psychiatric textbooks and some psychology ones. But Kallman's methodology was questionable to say the least. For one thing, Kallman performed all of the diagnoses in the study himself, while being well-aware of what it was that he was trying to prove. In many cases, he diagnosed members of the family as schizophrenic or as schizoid personalities simply on the basis of anecdotes or case notes – some of these family members had even been dead for twenty years at the time of the study! And he made sure that his diagnoses fitted perfectly the model which he was putting forward.

On the basis of his theory, Kallman argued vigorously for the compulsory sterilisation of schizophrenics: a policy which was soon put into practice in Nazi Germany. Not long afterwards, schizophrenics were sent to the concentration camps. So a single, seriously biased piece of 'scientific' research, performed by someone with strong opinions and in a way which guaranteed that those opinions would appear to be substantiated, directly caused the deaths of thousands of mentally ill people.

The dodgy methodology of the hereditarian side usually remains unchallenged. But dubious scientific practices pervade the history of this theory, and even result in the rewriting of apparently contradictory findings. The twin study conducted by Newman, Freeman and Holzinger, for instance, showed little evidence of heredity. But its statistical outcomes were systematically 'corrected' by hereditarians, until a relatively low correlation in the region of 0.6 was reworked so much that it became a high correlation of 0.8 – and the study was then extensively cited as evidence for the hereditarian argument.

Other studies of separated identical twins relied heavily on twins who were only nominally separated: the usual pattern was that one would be brought up by its biological mother and the other by a relative; they frequently went to the same schools and spent time together. Those studies which were not amenable to being reworked to support the hereditarian argument were simply never cited, and became forgotten.

Moreover, there are powerful lobbies at work in this area. When Cyril Burt's work on inherited intelligence was shown to be fabricated, the hereditarians simply closed ranks and insisted that there was still lots of other evidence. But, as Leon Kamin showed, if that other evidence is chased up, it isn't very convincing at all. Burt's work was so influential, and other studies so ambivalent in their evidence, that actually very little is left. Even today, we find certain people attempting to restore Burt's credibility, despite the fact that only very few aspects of the evidence for fraud have been exonerated, and the overwhelming evidence still remains.

My point is this: if the case for the hereditarians is as clear-cut as they maintain, why do they need to engage in questionable scientific practices? Surely, if the theory is valid, it will produce clear-cut evidence: these machinations should be unnecessary. The reason, of course, is that these people are not purveying scientific theory, but ideology. It is a political perspective with very direct political implications: it legitimises the inequalities of society by arguing that these arise from inherited differences; and negates attempts to create a better society by implying that they are doomed to failure from the start.

Not all of the evidence, of course, results from deliberate fraud or misrepresentation. But other studies also have serious methodological weaknesses. In the case of adoption studies, for instance, these mean that they imply a closer connection with biological parents than is really the case. This argument centres around the use of correlation coefficients. A correlation coefficient indicates how far two variables vary together. But it doesn't tell us anything about the actual value of each set of figures. In almost all of the adoption studies which used formal IQ tests (some of them simply took the mother's educational level instead), the actual value of the adopted child's IQ was closer to that of the adoptive mother, sometimes by as much as 20 IQ points. But the use of correlational measures meant that it looked as though there was a closer relationship with the biological parent.

IQ testing

And all of these studies, of course, rest on the assumption that the IQ test is a precision instrument which can accurately reflect an individual's intelligence. Differences of just a couple of points are treated as if they were precise data, although the reliability coefficients of the tests indicate that much larger differences would occur by chance alone. IQ tests are not precise instruments, nor are they accurate indicators of intelligence.

As Stephen J. Gould showed in *The Mismeasure of Man*, ever since the first battery IQ tests were developed, they have been culturally biased in ways which ensure that white middle-class individuals will score most highly. The first systematic IQ tests were used by US immigration authorities to control entrance to the United States at the beginning of the twentieth century. They were unashamedly racist, asking such questions as 'The number of a Kaffir's legs is: 2,4,6,8?'. They also asked would-be immigrants questions about American baseball heroes, and in the non-verbal tests which supposedly allowed for language difficulties they were expected to be familiar with artefacts from American culture, like being able to draw in the missing horn from a phonograph, or place a ball in the hand of a man in a bowling alley. (No marks, incidentally, given for placing it in the hand of a woman in the same picture!)

The bias inherent in these tests was extreme, but many researchers have demonstrated how later IQ tests, too, discriminate strongly against certain populations, such as black Americans or people from working-class backgrounds. In America they have been successfully challenged in the courts: Judge Peckham, in 1979, ruled that education authorities who used IQ tests to place black children in special schools for the mentally retarded were discriminating against ethnic minority students, because standardised intelligence tests are racially and culturally biased, and because they were being misused in this diagnostic role.

There are other forms of social bias in these tests too. In the WISC, for example, which is one of the most widely-used individual IQ tests in Britain and in America, children are asked: 'What is the correct thing to do if you find a stamped, addressed letter in the street?' It is marked as follows: 2 marks for saying 'post it', or 'give it to a postman'; 1 mark for saying 'give it to a policeman, teacher, or someone in authority'. But no marks at all for saying 'open it'. It's a measure of social conformity, not a measure of intelligence.

All these, of course, are factors which are completely ignored by those putting forward the hereditarian theory of IQ. When Arthur Jensen revived the race and IQ controversy, in 1969, he argued that because American blacks scored an average of 15 IQ points lower than American whites, they were therefore lower in intelligence and should receive special schooling accordingly.

Jensen's arguments relied almost entirely on Burt's statistics; and we know how reliable they were. But the reason why he achieved such acclaim was because he was putting a pseudo-scientific gloss on a political issue: legitimising the views of racists that black people were 'inferior', and providing a rationalisation for those who were objecting to their children attending mixed schools. His views are still quoted as 'proof' of the supposed inferiority of blacks in National Front propaganda.

It is worth noting, incidentally, that ever since the very first IQ tests were developed, girls have scored more highly than boys, and women than men; but this mean difference in IQ scoring was simply dealt with by adjusting the population norms of the tests. A girl has to answer more questions correctly than a boy to get the same IQ score. If the IQ difference between blacks and whites was so important, why didn't they simply adjust the population norms? Three guesses...

FIGURE 12.1

Eugenics

But all of this hides the main issue. When we are looking at the nature-nurture debate on intelligence, the key word is one which appears only peripherally in the textbooks: *eugenics*. Eugenic theory was developed by Francis Galton at the end of the nineteenth century, and it is directly linked with the concept of inherited intelligence. In his paper *Hereditary Genius*, Galton described a number of families of eminent Victorians (he was a cousin of Charles Darwin). He then argued that, since intelligence clearly ran in families, it must therefore be inherited, overlooking entirely the idea that families also provide environments for their children to grow up in. Galton went on to observe with alarm that the 'lower classes' in society were breeding prolifically, and argued that this would result in a lowering of the overall intelligence of the nation, or of the race. Therefore, he argued, in the interests of the future progression of the human race, inferior people, such as those of low intelligence, should be sterilised to prevent them from having children.

All this might simply seem like, and is often presented as, a rather undesirable eccentricity in someone who was otherwise a respected academic figure. But it actually goes much further than that. Galton's ideas were far from eccentric. Indeed, they became so widely accepted and so deeply ingrained into society that laws which enforced compulsory sterilisation of those with low IQs were passed by several American states. Moreover, these laws continued to be implemented – for example, in the state of Virginia – right up until 1972.

Eugenic principles of weeding out undesirables to encourage genetic 'progress' also underlay the massive extermination programme conducted by the Third Reich, and the American sterilisation programmes were taken by Hitler as a model of desirable social reform. The Nazis linked eugenics with a spurious form of evolutionary theory, which held that human races had 'evolved' in a sequential order, with each stage being more advanced than the last. In this model, for which no scientific evidence was ever found, blacks were considered to be the most 'primitive', and the Aryan race the most 'advanced'. For the Nazis, therefore, 'miscegenation', or racial mixing, was a serious crime. Following Galton's eugenic principles, they saw it as weakening the genetic stock of the human being and hindering the ultimate evolution of the 'superman'. They were particularly hostile to Jewish people, because they saw them as being genetically inferior but close enough to Aryan stock to make 'miscegenation' a serious problem.

As we have seen, Kallman's argument for sterilisation of schizophrenics was also based on eugenic principles. So, far from eugenics being an academic theory, or the eccentricities of a Victorian academic, it has been directly responsible for the deaths of millions of people and the compulsory sterilisation of tens of thousands more. Francis Galton's eugenic ideas reverberated throughout the twentieth century, and are still propagated by the National Front and similar neo-fascist organisations. The groundwork for them lies in nativist arguments: the theory of inherited intelligence. But, as we have seen, these are fraught with problems.

We see this question of ideology coming up again when we take a look at one of the most influential social biologists of the twentieth century: the ethologist Konrad Lorenz. Lorenz was an Austrian, a member of the Nazi party, and a supporter of the Final Solution, which was the Nazis' euphemism for the extermination of the Jewish people. Lorenz developed a theory of innate aggression which became widely accepted in both psychology and biology. In it, he portrayed aggression as an innate quality in all animals, including human beings, which had to have an outlet because it was continually building up. It could be sublimated into sports, he believed, or into other competitive activities, but its existence was the reason why human beings had wars and territorial disputes.

Effectively, as you can see, Lorenz was restating the Hobbesian belief in the anti-social nature of humanity, and this time giving it apparent credibility by citing instances of animal behaviour which appeared to support it. By presenting aggression as a biological inevitability, Lorenz legitimised the aggressive expansionism of Nazi Germany, and by setting it in an evolutionary context, he legitimised their victimisation of weaker members of society as being for the social good – as a form of 'survival of the fittest'.

Lorenz's reductionist explanation for wars would not be shared by many people nowadays, although it was in keeping with its time. It is commonly accepted that wars have an economic basis rather than a personal one: if human beings were so 'naturally' aggressive, they would hardly need the massive propaganda machine which is involved in any war. In fact, just look around and you'll find that human beings, by and large, tend to try very hard to avoid aggressive confrontations – most people will run a mile rather than say 'no' to someone's face. When people do become violent or aggressive, we know that there is always some other factor involved: either they are under pressure from some other source or they are in a highly aroused physiological state. Lorenz's theory of aggression, however, makes much more sense once we know about his connections with the Nazi party.

As those who have studied the psychology of emotion will realise, what we do inherit is a nervous system which can become aroused; but how we interpret that arousal depends on our circumstances. The same situation may provoke very different reactions, depending on a number of factors. And people who experience low levels of personal stress or frustration become demonstrably less aggressive. But if we see aggression as an inherited drive, then we don't need to ask any embarrassing questions about why people are feeling frustrated, or what has brought them to this point: we can simply ignore street rioters or terrorists, without having to ask ourselves what it is really all about. Politically speaking, the concept of inherited aggression is an extremely useful one.

Problems of nativist argument

One major problem of making a rigid distinction between nature and nurture is that it ignores how organisms actually develop – which is why geneticists have never been as enamoured with the idea as psychologists were. The fundamental distinction which geneticists make is between genotype and phenotype. The genotype is the inherited 'blueprint' which is represented in the individual's gene pattern, and which has been passed on from both parents. The phenotype, on the other hand, is the characteristics which the individual actually develops as they mature.

It is not possible for the genotype to determine what a person is like. The person emerges as a result of the interaction between genotype and experience: if we look at a child or at a grown person, what we see is the phenotype, not the genotype. Someone may inherit tall stature and blond hair, for instance, and this may result in her being treated socially in a manner which is different from those with short stature and dark hair. In that sense, the genotype has been influential in her experience, since it has helped to produce the phenotype that people are responding to. But the nature of that influence will vary depending upon the kind of society in which she lives: the sub-culture within that society, the family relationships which she has. One person with that kind of geno-type may grow up confident, poised and socially reassured; another may become timid, lacking confidence and unwilling to attract attention.

D. O. Hebb tried to bring this point home as far back as 1949, with his 'egg' analogy. He pointed out that if we take the genotype away, there is no egg; but if we remove the warm supporting environment, the egg dies. Nature cannot be regarded as distinct from nurture; there is a dialectical interrelationship between the two such that each is totally dependent on the other. Nor does it make any sense to claim that the egg is 80 per cent inherited or 60 per cent, or any other percentage: each side is equally essential.

Nativist arguments are by definition reductionist. By saying that some aspect of development is caused by the genes, any further explanation is precluded: there isn't anything else to say. It leads to researchers, and politicians, ignoring – or regarding as non-signif-icant – the other influences, agencies or developments which are influential in human life. It focuses on one level of explanation and simply ignores the rest. I have dealt with the problems of reduc-tionism as a form of argument elsewhere (see Chapter 1), and, as with other examples, it's the lack of consideration of other levels of explanation which is the most important problem. By ignoring all other levels, nativist arguments produce a completely static model of the human being: one which presents human nature as fixed and unchangeable.

And what these arguments do, therefore, is act to support the status quo. The view that intelligence is fixed means that there's no need to do anything about better education for those who are 'less capable'. The idea that mental illness is inherited means that we don't have to look at the social pressures that people are under. And the idea that people are innately aggressive means that we obviously need to keep them under tight control with strict law and order.

What is particularly revealing in all of this, of course, is the way that exposés make so little difference. When Burt was shown to be a fraud, the hereditarians kept on arguing their points regardless; Marshall's paper in the BPS *Bulletin* which showed the method-ological problems of Kallman's studies went almost completely ignored; Kamin's criticisms of the adoption and family studies in intelligence have been similarly ignored. It is a powerful paradigm, which commands a great deal of media support, and its power lies precisely in its political overtones. As we have seen, these are not just academic theories.

Nazi Germany showed us the logical outcome of a society organised purely around nativist principles. We should take warning from this. An interactionist perspective, on the other hand, looks to improving social conditions to facilitate social change. And this leads us to one of the most important questions: are human beings fixed, or can they change? A wide body of evidence shows that they can. The nativist view, though, is that change is impossible, or at least only to a limited extent. I do not, personally, find any adequate evidence for this view.

But we don't need to choose between nativism and empiricism: it is our phenotypes, not our genotypes, which we use to interact with the world. All of us have an inherited biology which channels us in certain directions: we are particularly sensitive to social signals from others, even from the cradle; we learn quickly; we use our hands rather than our feet to manipulate objects, and so on. These are aspects of our species biology. There are biological dimensions to individual differences too: some babies have a more labile autonomic nervous system than others, and so are more easily aroused; others respond more quickly to novel stimuli than others; some babies like to be cuddled and some don't.

But these are differences in temperament. How they actually become expressed varies, depending on how we interact with our social and physical environment. Someone with a highly labile autonomic nervous system might grow up to be an energetic, charismatic public speaker; or an anxious, nervous introvert. Someone who enjoys novelty may become a curious inventor, or an avid fashion-follower. The genotype doesn't determine the phenotype, although it may point us in certain directions rather than others. The potential for growth, development and change, though, always remains.

Chapter 13

The 'Magic' of Sociobiology*

When E. O. Wilson's *Sociobiology: The New Synthesis* was first launched in 1975, its arrival was greeted with immense excitement on the part of the media, as well as within the academic world. As a theory, it provided a comprehensive – even global – set of 'explanations' of the human condition and human societies, in a respectably tentative, academic way. Moreover, it had the ultimate claim to credibility: the theory was, we were told, scientific – drawing on evidence from experts in the worlds of biology and ethology, and presenting its conclusions in a suitably scientific manner, using mathematical models derived from game theory to present a convincing series of numbers, tables and diagrams. The large, coffee-table-style book was an instant hit, resulting in articles in such publications as *Reader's Digest, House and Garden*, and many others. At the same time, it became widely read within the academic world and, while debated over hotly by many, was readily accepted by very many more working academics.

The book's influence was immense. Sociobiological explanations of behaviour became common in the popular media. While articles drawing on biological origins for human behaviour have always been around, Richard Dawkins replaced Desmond Morris as the mass media's guru of biological determinism. In the academic field, some biologists even claimed that sociobiology was the third phase of evolutionary theory: that all current thinking must, inevitably, fit into this framework. (Others, needless to say, disagreed.)

Sociobiological arguments also crept into psychology: social psychologists toyed with sociobiological explanations for problems such as why people seem to lend money more readily to relatives than to friends; right-wing psychologists put forward

* I am indebted to Steven Rose for his helpful comments and criticisms of an earlier version of this paper. This article originally appeared in *Psychology Teaching* (1986) (2): 2–16.

sociobiologically-based theories to 'explain' racism and xenophobia in society, on the basis of genetic similarity. In short, the celebrations at the launch of E. O. Wilson's book were well-justified – it was indeed a highly influential and best-selling theory, with even Dawkins's small popular paperback *The Selfish Gene* to carry the message further to the clamouring masses.

Sociobiological theory

But what of the theory itself? Sociobiology attempts to explain both human and animal behaviour by placing them firmly within an evolutionary context. Wilson assumes (or rather, states explicitly) that all animal behaviour is directly coded in the genes. He went on to assert that both animal and human behaviour are directly concerned not with the survival of the individual but with the survival of that individual's genes. Animals are considered to be simply biological mechanisms by which genes perpetuate themselves – and so are human beings. Although the extrapolation to human behaviour was limited to just one tentative final chapter of the book *Sociobiology*, Wilson's later publication *On Human Nature* showed that he saw human beings as following the same 'genetic imperatives'.

Wilson formulated sociobiological theory as a result of his research into ant societies, in which he had observed that individuals would often sacrifice their own survival to ensure the survival of others. Since this could not be explained using conventional evolutionary models, Wilson proposed that what was important was the fact that close relatives shared a high proportion of their genes. This mirrored observations by the biologist J. B. S. Haldane, who, reputedly, during a conversation about altruism in a pub, made some rapid calculations on the back of an envelope, and announced, 'I will lay down my life for two brothers or eight cousins' (Gould, 1978). Since brothers have half of their genes in common, and cousins have an eighth, these figures theoretically expressed the minimal requirement for an individual to ensure that their genes would survive.

This version of evolutionary theory, therefore, was genetic determinism in its most extreme form. Rather than being seen as acting to maximise their own individual survival, individual animals (and humans) were now seen as acting to maximise genetic survival. As a result, even altruistic actions – previously ignored by genetic determinists, who construed individual survival purely in terms of conflict and aggression – could be explained as manifestations of the 'selfish gene', through the concept of kin selection – and were.

Despite its popularity, however, sociobiology made a number of claims to academic validity which do not really stand up to a good close scrutiny. It has a scientific veneer, but sociobiology is not an academically sound theory resting firmly on scientific evidence. Rather, sociobiology, as a system of explanation, is fundamentally both magical and unscientific.

These terms need some explanation. Firstly, what do I mean by 'magical'? When I say that, in terms of its explanations, a framework is magical, I am using a set of criteria concerning magical, as opposed to scientific, explanation, which can be stated fairly explicitly as follows:

1   Magical explanations do not rely on material evidence ('facts').
2   Magical explanations rely on the invocation of axioms – mystical formulae – which are used to account for events which occur.
3   By virtue of these mystical formulae, magical explanations for events preclude further investigation – they are considered to be totally self-sufficient explanations which do not require further questioning.

Sociobiology, as an explanatory system, conforms to all three of these criteria.

When I say that sociobiology is unscientific, I am also drawing on a set of criteria concerning the nature of scientific explanation, which can be stated as follows:

1   Scientific explanation is fundamentally materialist in nature, resting on empirical data.
2   Scientific explanations take the form of theories, which are put forward as possible explanations for events, but which are refutable in the event of alternative empirical data becoming available.
3   Scientific explanations give rise to predictions, which can be tested against reality as further investigation of the theory.

Although these criteria may be perceived as slightly idealised, in terms of the actual practice of science by scientists (see, for example,

Kuhn, 1962), they nonetheless summarise a set of assumptions held about science, by those within it, as well as those outside. Sociobiology, despite its claims to scientific respectability, does not conform to these criteria, and so must be regarded, in these terms, as unscientific.

Sociobiological explanation

The first argument against sociobiological explanation is that it does not rest itself on empirical data, as currently available. Rather, it selects its data from among a wealth of investigations, choosing only that which confirms its own arguments, and ignoring or dismissing the rest with little justification.

The primary evidence of sociobiological explanation is ethological observations of animal behaviour. In one form or another these have been in vogue for the whole of the twentieth century, and a considerable bank of studies has accumulated. In *Sociobiology*, Wilson drew heavily on his own studies of slavery in ants, and, following the well-established traditions of such writers as Robert Ardrey and Desmond Morris, generalised his conclusions to the rest of the animal kingdom, including, by implication, humans. Having shown that ants, bees and wasps were prepared to commit individual suicide in defence of their colonies, he explained this in terms of their 'genes' surviving in the bodies of those relatives who were successfully defended. He then stated that the same mechanisms operate – or 'appear' to operate, in higher mammals, and went on to argue that the genetic explanation must also be true of humans on the grounds that human beings, too, must have evolved in small, closely related communities.

It can be seen that there are many flaws in this line of argument, not the least of which being the question of what the mammalian brain is for, which I shall discuss further later on in this chapter. But a very real question is, 'Why ants?' Wilson claimed to be arguing from an evolutionary perspective, and yet ignored, for his most fundamental arguments, studies of animals which are evolutionarily much closer to the human being. While it wouldn't necessarily be true to say that insects are as phylogenetically as far away from humans as you can get, it is certainly true to say that their evolution has proceeded along very different lines from that of the mammals. Behavioural mechanisms which appear to parallel those of mammals are not necessarily the same at all. Analogy doesn't mean homology – looking similar doesn't mean being the same thing.

Evidence from the higher mammals in sociobiological reasoning tends to be rather conspicuous by its absence, with sociobiologists much preferring to take their examples from insects, birds and fish. When mammals are used, the evidence is very highly selective indeed – an example quoted by Dawkins on surrogate parenting, for instance, rests on precisely two cases: that male mice secrete a pheromone which causes females who are pregnant with offspring not related to that male to abort; and that new male lions joining a pride will sometimes kill the young cubs. He then uses this to support an elaborate argument about male control of female reproduction, the advantages of a long courtship (making sure the female isn't already pregnant by somebody else), monogamy, and so on and so forth. On those observations of mammals adopting, or caring for, non-related individuals, such as with baboon 'aunts', or mongooses, his only comment is that the rule must be 'misfiring'.

In other words, if it doesn't fit the explanation, it doesn't really count. However, the diversity of behavioural patterns and social organisational strategies in the animal kingdom is vast. To dismiss what is turning out to be a very large number of ethological studies in such a summary fashion cannot be acceptable in a theory which purports to have global application. Such a form of argument becomes justifiable in sociobiological terms, I contend, because sociobiology does not form a scientific theory. Rather, it forms a series of assertions about what 'ought' to be, rather than what 'is'.

Its proponents, of course, hotly dispute this. Both Wilson and Dawkins issue warnings that straightforward descriptions of what 'is' should not be taken as justifying their continuance. At the same time, though, they make it quite clear that they regard any attempts to be different as a struggle against our biological nature. The 'natural' tendency of the human being, according to the sociobiologists, is towards such endearing qualities as xenophobia, aggressive territoriality, rigid sexual distinctions, and altruism only as long as it has some sort of pay-off for the altruist. Other forms of human societies may be possible, they admit, but they give the distinct impression that this would be at a biological cost rather akin to walking around on all fours.

When they are faced with their arguments in this sort of form, it is not uncommon for sociobiologists to retreat into the defence that they are not claiming that genes determine human behaviour, only that they determine a possible range of human behaviours. But any kind of behaviour which has been shown by human beings must be biologically possible, otherwise we wouldn't be able to do it. Flying without artificial aids, for instance, is notably absent in the repertoire of recorded human achievements. But stable forms of human society, or instances of human behaviour which do not conform to the assumptions made within sociobiology, do exist and have existed in the past.

Once again we are back to the question of selectivity of evidence, and it is notable that the evidence from human societies selected by sociobiological theorists just 'happens' to coincide with assumptions about human nature considered appropriate for Western industrial society, even though they are totally inappropriate for many other cultures in the world. As an 'explanation' for the ills of Western society, it fits the bill admirably: of course new step-parents find it difficult adjusting to their new children! Nothing to do with different family practices or beliefs – it's simply that they are going against their 'selfish gene', which is pressurising them to do away with any rival offspring!

Of course, the clear implication is that it would have been much better if the original parents had never divorced in the first place. These fundamentally prescriptive and subtly moralistic assumptions of sociobiology permeate the arguments. Often, they reveal themselves most clearly not in the actual statements made but in the language selected to make them in. For example, starting from tentative introductions, replete with caveats, Richard Dawkins goes on to argue a chain of reasoning which inevitably ends in the word 'must': 'We must expect lies and deceit, and selfish exploitation of communication to arise whenever the interests of the genes of different individuals converge...[so]...we must expect that children will deceive their parents, that husbands will cheat on wives, and that brother will lie to brother' (Dawkins, 1976, p. 70).

As I previously remarked, these statements are not made without caveats: at another stage in the book Dawkins states, 'If there is a human moral to be drawn, it is that we must teach our children altruism, for we cannot expect it to be part of their biological nature' (Dawkins, 1976, p. 149). Nonetheless, they are made, and moreover made in a way which presents them as the logical outcomes of a process of scientific reasoning. And the negative assertions far outweigh the caveats, in linguistic power as well as in frequency.

This brings us on to the question of sociobiological methodology. In most sciences, the accepted methods of scientific enquiry are to do with deriving some kind of hypothesis from a theory, and then testing out that hypothesis by some form of experimentation or observational study. This, however, is not the case with sociobiology. Rather than being predictive in its approach, and formulating hypotheses which can then be tested, sociobiological argument is retrospective in nature. It starts with an assertion about some form of behaviour – in the case of humans, one which is supposed to be 'universal' (although that in many cases is open to question). From there, it proceeds to 'explain' that behaviour, firstly by postulating a gene which could account for its occurrence, and then by seeking an evolutionary story which shows how that gene could be shown to be adaptive.

It can be seen from this that, providing the theorist is inventive enough, any form of behaviour can be 'explained', but the circularity of its reasoning is striking. There is no way of ever refuting these arguments, since they are entirely circular: the 'universal' behaviour is seen as both the effect and the cause of the 'gene'. If an important characteristic of scientific theories is that they should be open to refutation, then a process which uses this form of methodology cannot be considered to be scientific, as it cannot be refuted. One is reminded of some psychoanalytic theories, also postulated as 'scientific' in an earlier time, and just as circular.

Sociobiology as magic

Rather than being a form of scientific investigation, sociobiological reasoning is actually much more akin to the magical axioms to 'explain' events. In sociobiology, the magical axiom is the 'gene', rather than the spell, or the curse, but as a general-purpose concept it is just as useful. When we examine how sociobiologists use the word 'gene', we can see that it bears little resemblance to the phenomenon investigated by geneticists – and indeed, some of the most vociferous criticisms of sociobiology have come from the field of genetics, rather than sociology or psychology.

Genes

In *The Selfish Gene*, having stated that: 'We can define a word how we like for our own purposes, provided we do so clearly and unambiguously' (Dawkins, 1976, p. 30), Dawkins defines a gene as a unit of natural selection. However, in genetic terms, a gene is a portion of chromosomal material which brings about a particular protein synthesis in the organism, and his comment about defining words is made precisely because he is not using the word with this meaning. A unit of natural selection may be something else altogether, and at the very least is likely to be a combination of genes rather than one specific one.

In other words, both Dawkins and Wilson take a word with a highly specific biological meaning, and use it with a very much vaguer, and ultimately indefinable (except circularly) meaning. What this strategy does is to give an apparently scientific precision to the theory, and therefore increases its apparent plausibility. But there is little scientific justification for doing so.

If one attempts to get specific about what a gene actually does, then the magical nature of the concept becomes even more apparent. No attempt is made to move from the level of protein synthesis to behaviour: such connections are taken for granted. If an organism carries the necessary genes for that particular behaviour, then that behaviour happens. The 'gene' does it, it seems, quite magically.

We are, however, as yet very far from an understanding of how neurochemistry and cognition interrelate, and our assumptions about these mechanisms are grossly immature. But one thing that we can say is that modern brain research is showing more and more evidence for a dialectical interrelationship between cognitions, environment and neurochemistry, in which each affects the other reciprocally. As a result, it is becoming clear that simplistic statements involving our biology 'causing' our behaviour don't hold up very well in real life. Perhaps it is just as well that sociobiology hasn't actually attempted to deal with this question, but it doesn't make their use of the word 'gene' any less magical.

Kin selection

The concept of kin selection, while perhaps being rather more specific in nature, also provides sociobiology with an opportunity to 'explain' anything, or pretty well anything, to do with human behaviour. Since human beings 'must' have evolved in small, closely related groups, any behaviour which involves humans being nice to one another can be seen as deriving from kin-oriented altruism, while any behaviour which involves humans being nasty to one another can be seen as direct evolutionary competition. Either way, it 'must' be controlled by the 'genes'. Heads I win, tails you lose.

Of course, if modern humans end up being nice to totally unrelated strangers, this is simply because they are applying the principle inappropriately. Wilson states that we should consider the possibility that '...altruistic behaviours will decline through the loss of group selection, a process that could spread over perhaps two or three centuries'. (Incidentally, the timescale here makes one wonder how fast Wilson thinks human beings reproduce, and, at least to me, reinforces my conviction that he sees evolution as a magical – certainly not gradual – event.)

There is much more that can be said about sociobiological reasoning. We could talk about its use of metaphor, for instance, which confuses any attempt at scientific interpretation of animal observation by using human analogies, often inappropriately. As Rose (1984) asked: just how does a 'totally captive, force-fed egg-bearing machine have any resemblance to Elizabeth 1 or Catherine the Great'? There is also the issue of reductionist explanation *per se*, but we looked at that in some detail in Chapter 1, and elsewhere in this book. I think that we have seen enough to be able to return to the original assertion, that sociobiology is magical and unscientific.

On the question of magical explanations, then, we have seen that sociobiology does not rest on material evidence, or at least only on highly selective versions of it. Its central concept, the gene, is not the one understood by geneticists, but is more of an axiom which is evoked as if it were an explanation. Because of the all-embracing nature of its explanatory constructs, it precludes further investigation, both of other causes of behaviour, and of processes within the individual which might give rise to specific behaviours. So in terms of the criteria outlined at the beginning of this chapter, it conforms well with magical belief-systems.

However, when we turn to scientific criteria, we find that sociobiological explanation rests on a process of reasoning by analogy rather than material evidence, that its 'explanations' are not refutable because it is all-embracing, and that it operates by retrospective deduction rather than by prediction. This hardly accords well with its claim to be a scientific theory.

Evolution and behaviour: an alternative view

It seems to me, and has done since my undergraduate days, that one problem which ethologists consistently fail to come to terms with is the question of what the brain is for. Lip-service is paid to the idea that the more complicated brain has developed because it helps the individual to adapt to its environment better, but the full implications of that idea are rarely explored.

In this argument, I am concerned primarily with the development of that part of the brain which shows its most striking development in the primates and cetaceans: the cerebrum. To be more specific, it is the question of the cerebral cortex which is the main focus of attention. If we draw up an approximate phylogenetic scale, ranking groups of species in terms of their relatedness to human beings, and excluding cetaceans, because we don't really know very much about their behaviour, we find a dramatic increase in the size of the cerebrum – and particularly in the cerebral cortex (Figure 13.1).

In fish and reptiles, the forebrain, the precursor of the cerebrum, is relatively small by comparison with other structures of the brain. In birds, it is the largest of the structures, but still not very large. With mammals, the cerebrum as we know it appears, and as we move through marsupials and higher mammals, to monkeys, then apes, then humans, we find a consistent and impressive development in its structure (Hubel, 1979). The surface of the cerebrum becomes larger and larger, convolutions appear, and the cerebral cortex comes to overshadow all the other brain structures. So an evolutionary theorist is faced with the question of why this should be. What function does this structure serve, that its development in phylogenetic terms should be so striking?

Many of the functions of the cerebral cortex are listed in the standard textbooks. We know that it mediates language in human beings, that it is involved with interpreting sensory information, although the primary decoding seems to take place elsewhere in the brain; that it initiates voluntary movement, although this also is coordinated elsewhere in the brain; that it is involved with our experience of emotions, in conjunction with other systems; and that it seems to be the main organ responsible for learning and memory, although other structures are involved in this as well. In short, the cerebral cortex seems to be a high-level information processor, which can control, coordinate and mediate the organism's interaction with the environment. Most importantly, it allows the organism to learn from its experience.

With the development of learning, an individual organism can adapt its behaviour to take account of new circumstances. All animals can learn to some extent, but it is clear that some can

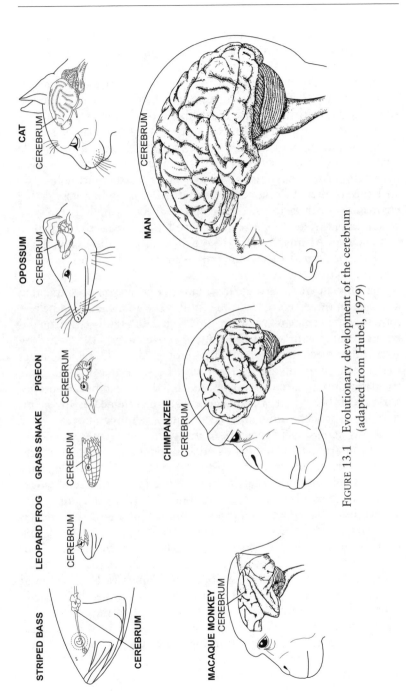

STRIPED BASS   LEOPARD FROG   GRASS SNAKE   PIGEON   OPOSSUM   CAT

CEREBRUM   CEREBRUM   CEREBRUM   CEREBRUM   CEREBRUM

CEREBRUM

MAN   CEREBRUM

CHIMPANZEE   CEREBRUM

MACAQUE MONKEY   CEREBRUM

FIGURE 13.1   Evolutionary development of the cerebrum (adapted from Hubel, 1979)

modify their behaviour to a greater extent than others – and those are the ones which have the more highly developed cerebral cortex. In evolutionary terms, of course, this confers a definite advantage to an animal which may be living in widely different environments. If you can adapt your behaviour to new circumstances rapidly, then you are more likely to survive.

Of course, if you happen to be a species living in a relatively stable environment, or with a social structure which maintains a stable environment for the key individuals, then this isn't likely to be very important. Ants may live in many places on the earth, but the structure of their colonies ensures that they maintain a very stable environment for their breeding females. Species which live in consistent habitats, as do many birds, also have little reason to evolve a high level of adaptability. (Note that in this discussion I am thinking of animal behaviour only – plants and bacteria are not featured in this argument!)

Learning, however, is only important as long as you do something about it. In other words, learning must result in a change in behaviour, so that in some way you are now acting differently than you did before. And if your behaviour patterns have already been fixed by some other mechanism, you will find a conflict – the same conflict that Lorenz and Tinbergen saw when they subjected fish and birds to inappropriate stimuli and elicited fixed, stereotyped responses from them. Behaviour which is genetically determined is, by definition, fixed, at least within any one individual, although it may evolve gradually across many generations into a different pattern.

We can argue that the phylogenetic development of the cerebral cortex in mammals represents a fundamental change in the acquisition of behavioural patterns. As we move higher up the phylogenetic scale (treat this idea with caution: it really doesn't imply that all evolution is aiming to produce human beings!), we find an increasing dependence on learned behaviour, and a decreasing reliance on inherited patterns of behaving. The increased size of the cerebral cortex allows for a greater emphasis on learning in the course of the individual's development. This goes hand in hand with *neoteny* – the tendency for species higher up the phylogenetic scale to be born at an increasingly early stage in their life cycles, which means that the young have a far longer period of dependency (during which they are learning all the time).

I am not implying here that genes have nothing to do with development. It is our genes, after all, which tell us to grow these highly convoluted brains. Rather I am suggesting that we see a progressive decrease in direct genetic control of behaviour, as we move higher up the phylogenetic scale. Moreover, this is a systematic evolutionary change with definite survival advantages for the individual. In some ways this is similar to Dawkins's idea that sometimes genes hold behaviour 'on a very long leash'. But I am also arguing that by the time you get to apes and humans, the leash has become so long that to talk of human behaviour as if it were genetically determined is just nonsense.

I think, also (though this is rather more tentative), that we can trace the gradual abdication of direct control of behaviour by the genes through a series of intermediate stages. We can see a gradual progression through fish, birds and mammals, from rigidly fixed behaviours (such as courtship rituals in sticklebacks and grebes), to generally fixed but modifiable behaviours (such as songbirds with regional 'accents' but the same basic pattern), to general tendencies towards certain forms of behaviours but which are increasingly modified by the individual's experience (such as emotional reactions in domestic pets).

Much work, recently, has shown how animals are prepared to engage in certain forms of learning rather than others. This ranges from Seligman's early observations of one-trial learning with regard to food to Gould and Marler's seminal discussion of how learning in bees, birds and other animals appears to be shaped according to the important features of that animal's environment. Bees learn to identify food sources by scent very easily indeed, they learn to identify them by colour somewhat less easily, and almost never learn them by shape. Birds respond most readily to sounds which have the physical characteristics of the adult song of their species. And humans respond most readily to sounds with the physical characteristics of the human voice.

We may also be seeing a progression, as the genes abdicate direct control of behaviour, in the amount of influence they exert. As Lorenz so convincingly demonstrated, young birds acquire their behaviours from their caretakers, but only during a particular period of time – a *sensitive period* (*née* critical). Other precocial species seem to do this too, but those with young which are dependent for longer periods of time seem to have a longer period of readiness for this kind of learning, and to base it more on interactions and transactions with the parent.

Indeed, by the time we come to look at human infants, we find that their most striking predispositions are towards sociability. The human infant seems to be born preprogrammed to respond to other human beings, and the attachment bond develops gradually through social interaction with others, not appearing in its full form until the infant is about seven months old. Through this prolonged period of dependency, the human gradually learns appropriate behaviours for the things which it will encounter in its environment, and the large cerebral cortex means that it will continue to learn throughout its life. In the retreat of direct genetic control of behaviour, to a generalised disposition to learn from one's caretakers, we see an increase in reliance on learned behaviours but without the evolutionary cost that learning from scratch by trial and error would produce.

I do not think that we need to postulate explanations for human behaviour in sociobiological terms. Why would we have such a large capacity for learning, if how we should behave was already fixed? It seems to me that if we are looking for an understanding of human beings in evolutionary terms, then we should do so in terms of the infant's tendency towards sociability, rather than looking at particular behaviours (usually specific to Western culture anyway), and then seeing if they are 'adaptive' and arguing that they must therefore be genetic. The wide variability of human behaviour has barely been explored – even within Western culture – and it is difficult to find 'universals' which will truly hold up for all human societies, let alone all human beings within those societies.

One further point, which I think is another very much undernoticed one. The human cerebral cortex has various areas which appear to have specific functions, although much of it is 'silent' – in other words, any functions specific to these areas are unknown. One of the areas with a specific role is known as the angular gyrus. Its function seems to be explicitly to do with reading. The angular gyrus is involved in passing information from the visual cortex to Wernicke's area, which is concerned with interpreting speech. In the process, it converts the visual message into the equivalent of auditory input. So we seem to have an area of the brain devoted specifically to reading.

My point is this: written language has not existed in human culture for long enough – let alone been universal – to have meant that we needed to evolve a special mechanism for it. The ability to read has never been the basis for species survival, and it is only in the past hundred years that mass literacy has even become a social goal. Literacy has, for the most part of human history, been restricted to a small elite. So how could we have evolved a physical part of the brain for reading?

However, this part of the brain exists. To me, this implies that what we inherit when we inherit the human brain is an organ which can adapt – physiologically – to entirely new types of situations. Colin Blakemore (1984) showed how the visual cells in the cortex can adopt modified functions in response to alternative environmental stimuli, and other animal studies have shown how brain weight may be increased by enriched environments (for example, Rosenzweig and Bennett, 1976). We have nuclei in the brain which give us the potential, and our experience either allows us to develop that potential or it doesn't.

If we think of the brain not so much in terms of structures which have evolved for a purpose but in terms of structures which give us the potential for learning and adapting our behaviour, we may be able to understand the wide variety of human behaviour a great deal better. Not only that, but we are also in a better position to understand the wide variability in animal behaviour, such as variable social organisations within the same species of mammal. Rather than having to ignore or dismiss studies of non-hierarchical organisation in baboon societies, or wide flexibility in the different behaviours of chimpanzees, we are in a position to make sense of them instead.

So why is sociobiology so popular?

One reason, of course, is that sociobology provides a very straightforward set of easy answers to questions, which, in a society based on instant gratification, is always appealing. By reducing human behaviour down to one level – the action of the genes – things seem to 'make sense', at least at first. As we saw in Chapter 1, reductionist explanations of human behaviour, by making things look very simple, have an appeal all of their own. By ignoring all the other levels on which a human can operate, they streamline the question enormously. The problem, though, is just how valuable their 'explanation' is, if, for instance, we wanted to do something daring like sort out the problem.

For example, if asked to explain wife-beating, a sociobiologist's answer is simple: the man is simply expressing the aggression natural towards someone who doesn't share the same genes. If, on the other hand, I was asked the same question, I could only answer on a whole series of levels: in terms of the patriarchal nature of power relationships in our society, socio-economic pressures and frustrations coming to a head; cognitive mismatches between the two of them in terms of their understanding of issues; and so on, which would take much longer and leave us with much more uncomfortable conclusions.

Another reason for sociobiology being so popular (you see, I even have to answer this using a whole series of levels), is that it falls into the well-established Western philosophical tradition of Cartesian dualism. Ever since Descartes put forward his view of the mind and the body as entirely separate things, and of the body as a machine, the Western world has adopted this line of thought – one reason, of course, why medicine has so much of a problem coming to terms with acupuncture and other holistic forms of medicine. The idea of the body as a machine blindly programmed by its selfish genes keeps our thinking well within this tradition. Add to this Descartes's insistence that all animal behaviour is totally mechanistic, stir in a bit of evolutionary theory – at least enough to say that humans are really 'only' animals – and we have a tasty brew, going down nicely with conventional ideas about human bodies and animal behaviour. So perhaps another reason for the popularity of sociobiology is that it doesn't really cause any uncomfortable rethinking or re-evaluation to go on.

We also have to look at just which sort of conclusions sociobiology produces. Again, we find that these are well in line with conventional Western assumptions about the nature of human beings (perhaps in this context I should say 'Man'), drawing as they do conclusions about patriarchy, xenophobia and aggression being 'natural' and inevitable. If sociobiological theory had ended with conclusions which suggested that all humans were 'naturally' cooperative and gentle – something which would be perfectly legitimate within the sociobiological method, and could be achieved simply by selecting different examples of animal behaviour, and different 'universals' of human societies – its popularity would have been negligible.

This is because ideas or theories which emphasise the basic sociability of the individual, rather than competitiveness or aggression, are rarely considered newsworthy. If one looks at the history of popularised scientific ideas, in contrast with actual scientific debate, one finds a distinct tendency for those which support the status quo to be taken up by the media, while contradictory theories, even if widely accepted in the academic world, are usually ignored. This, too, tells us something about the socio-political nature of these arguments.

The final reason I shall put forward for the popularity of sociobiology is to do with the 'Zeitgeist' – the spirit of the times. There are some topics – child-rearing is one, animal behaviour is another – which are, or at least seem to be, particularly susceptible to reflecting social and economic changes. Different theories arise at different times, and always when the economic climate seems ripe for them. So during the latter part of the Victorian period we had Spencer's Social Darwinism – 'nature red in tooth and claw' – which was used to justify the survival of the fittest in economic terms, and the neglect and abuse of poorer members of society.

During the 1960s, with an expanding economy and a growing social awareness, we had ethological theories which emphasised group cooperation through dominance hierarchies and the like. With the gradual rise of Thatcherism in Britain, and Reaganism in America, the harsher economic climate produced theories which concentrated on each looking after their own and ignoring other members of the species, as reflected in the idea of kin selection. Of course, this is not why Wilson wrote *Sociobiology*, but it does help us to account for why sociobiological theory became so popular, given its scientific weaknesses. A theory that accords with the mood of the times is a theory that people are ready to accept, perhaps far less critically than they might otherwise have done.

As I said earlier, I do not believe that we need to look to sociobiology for an adequate understanding of human, or even higher mammal, behaviour. Moreover, the nature of the conclusions it draws are more than simply invalid scientifically – in a social context they legitimise and make acceptable ideas which are not only misleading about the potential and nature of human beings, but also ultimately repressive. I do not believe that we have yet begun to explore human potential, and in that context, adopting repressive theories which don't even have scientific validity as a saving grace is entirely counter-productive, if we really are trying to understand the human being.

Chapter 14

Some Cognitive Implications of Human Social Evolution*

It is entirely accepted in the scientific community that human beings have evolved as social animals. This has profound implications, yet its cognitive consequences are rarely explored. If we are to understand these consequences, we need to begin by considering the demands which such evolution makes on cognition. In this chapter, I aim to show how a number of different research strands come together to illuminate distinctive aspects of human cognition. Research into different aspects of animal learning shows us how such learning is adaptive and multi-level in nature; and research into different areas of human psychology shows how our social adaptation carries significant implications for the understanding of human cognition.

The chapter brings together many different areas of research, and in an article of this length it would be impracticable to attempt to survey each one in detail. I have therefore chosen to refer to each area using 'classic' references which opened up those areas for other researchers. The overall insights of these older papers have not been refuted. However, subsequent research in each of these areas has almost always resulted in those initial insights being extended and refined by other researchers. The references given here are not, therefore, intended to form a detailed catalogue of current research. Instead, they are intended to provide an overview of fundamental insights in different research areas, which can be brought together in a meaningful sense to aid our overall theoretical understanding of the human mind.

* This article originally appeared as Hayes, N. (1999) 'Some cognitive implications of human social evolution', *Cognitive Systems*, 5(2): 123–35. Reproduced by permission.

Studies of animal learning in one form or another can throw light on the evolutionary shaping of human cognitive processes. So I shall begin by exploring four aspects of the evolution of cognition in terms of what we have learned from animal studies, and then go on to consider how these four aspects manifest themselves in human cognition.

Animal learning

The four aspects of animal cognitive evolution which are of particular interest here are the issue of adaptation and what it means in cognitive terms; the matter of critical and sensitive periods and their roles as mediators of learning; the question of preparedness in learning; and research into the various levels of learning.

Adaptation

It is invidious to view evolution as a progression towards the human being. Evolution is a series of adaptations to environmental circumstance, with no particular goal and no direction except in retrospect. Bearing that in mind, however, retrospective analysis of how certain characteristics have developed, and the evolutionary functions which made them an advantage, can be a valuable research tool.

Every organ in the body has a function, and that function has an evolutionary history which is all to do with helping an animal to survive. The nervous system is no exception. It enables the animal to produce behaviour which is appropriate to its environment, and which thereby facilitates that animal's survival. That's what it is for, and that's why it evolved. If survival requires increasingly complex behaviour, then an increasingly complex nervous system is required to control, regulate or shape it.

Acquiring an increasingly complex nervous system means that the animal acquires the ability to learn. This has powerful evolutionary implications. Learning is a function of the nervous system, and it has the direct advantage that it enables behaviour to become adapted within the lifetime of a single individual, instead of across generations. Such adaptation may be relatively minimal: an animal which operates in a consistent environment will not need to learn novel behaviours very often. But one which operates in a consistently changing environment faces more challenge.

We may be able to detect how these pressures have operated through a comparative examination of brain structures in different species. There, it is possible to trace some significant evolutionary steps. The transition from an aquatic environment to one on land, for example, was a move into an environment with more inconsistency and variation, and this is reflected in the difference in brain structure between fish and land animals. Thermoregulation and the ability to be active independently of external energy sources opened up another wave of environmental variation, and the brain's evolution to deal with those increasing demands is reflected in its structure (Hubel, 1979).

The most variable environment of all is that which is dependent on the activities and reactions of other animals, as well as on changes in the physical environment. Such dependency may arise because of complex sociability, or it may be an outcome of being a predator. Or both. But we can see the difference in brain development which occurs in tandem with these evolutionary influences (see figure 13.1). It is the role of the nervous system to make sure that what the animal does is appropriate to its environment. That's what adaptation is all about.

Critical and sensitive periods

Producing behaviour which is appropriate to the environment isn't a simple either-or between inherited and learned behaviour. Instead, we have a continuum, with inherited fixed action patterns at one extreme, and open learning of totally novel behaviours at the other. How an animal goes about acquiring appropriate behaviour may be through inheritance, through learning, or through any number of intermediate stages.

At one extreme, we have the fixed action patterns studied by Lorenz (1950) and Tinbergen (1951) in fish and seabirds. Many of these responses appear to be almost entirely inherited, appearing in response to relatively simple environmental stimuli –although, as Hailman (1969) showed, even purely inherited behaviours like these do improve with practice.

One step further on, we have behaviours which are mainly inherited, but modified by environmental experience. For example, Marler and Tamura (1964) showed how white-crowned sparrows reared in isolation do produce a basic version of their species' song when they are adult – implying that the song has been inherited. But this version is very crude, and lacks the regional variations, or 'accents', which birds of this species normally pick up from their parents.

Other behaviours are learned, rather than inherited, but their learning is heavily constrained by genetic processes. Studies of imprinting in precocial animals show that a young duckling can imprint on a human, or even an artefact. But that imprinting only occurs during a critical period, and in very specific situations (Sluckin, 1964). Effectively, the duckling will imprint on a large, distinctive (which usually means moving) object which it has been able to follow around for a period of at least ten minutes. Imprinting is even more likely if the large moving object makes familiar sounds – sounds which the chick has experienced while still in the egg (Hess, 1972). These conditions and constraints serve to narrow down the possibility of inappropriate learning: in the wild, the only thing likely to satisfy all of these criteria would be the mother duck. Here, genetic and environmental factors work together to ensure an evolutionarily appropriate outcome.

There are critical periods – developmental stages during which a certain type of learning must take place – and there are sensitive periods, during which an organism is particularly inclined to learn specific things. Sensitive periods are more flexible: it is possible for that particular type of learning to take place outside the period, but it is more likely to happen during that time. A sensitive period is another step back, away from direct genetic control of the behaviour, to a genetic predisposition which renders appropriate learning more likely (Hinde, 1987). It is part of a continuum: a gradual transition from the inheritance of fixed behaviour patterns adapted to consistent environmental demands to the ability to adapt behaviour to the demands of a variable environment.

Preparedness in learning
There is also the matter of what an animal learns. Some skills, for example, are more important than others in the matter of survival. Learning to avoid food which is poisonous is rather an essential skill; locating alternative routes between A and B may be a little less immediate for some animals, but may have direct survival value if you are a rabbit. Similarly, being able to distinguish between one or three approaching predators may have survival value in terms of selecting the best avoidance strategy, but being able to distinguish between seven and nine may not – in both cases, there are a lot of them. So, while we find many animal species able to count to three, those able to count beyond that number are very rare indeed.

Evolutionary pressures have shaped the nature of learning, as well as whether it takes place. Animals, including humans, learn some things more readily than others: they are powerfully prepared, through evolution, to undertake learning which has direct survival value; and consistently less prepared to undertake learning which has no or little relevance. Again, this is not an either-or matter: Gould and Marler's studies of preparedness in various species showed how bees, for example, learn very readily to respond to scents, particularly floral ones (Gould and Marler, 1987). They also learn fairly readily to respond to colours, although not as quickly as they learn scents; but they take much longer to learn to identify a food source by shape. They can do it in the end, but it needs five or six times as many learning trials than it does if scent is the distinctive stimulus.

This isn't just about learning through direct conditioning. A number of comparative researchers have shown how it applies to imitative learning, too. Animals, and birds, are particularly ready to imitate behaviours which have a strong survival component, and they will often learn these simply because of seeing other members of their species showing the behaviour. Gould and Marler (1987) discussed this in relation to birds and mobbing behaviour, but there are many other examples. The culturally transmitted food-washing behaviour of Japanese macaques has been much discussed; but it is no accident that this particular behaviour concerns food – an area where preparedness to learn is particularly powerful.

Being less prepared to learn, however, is not the same as being unable to learn. Some species, of which humans are the most apparent, show an unexpected capacity for additional learning with no obvious survival benefits. This may mean, of course, that we simply don't understand the subtleties of evolutionary pressures and there are hidden survival benefits to all learning. But the more usual explanation is that being especially ready to learn things which relate to survival does not make that the only learning possible. Rather, it is to assert that survival-oriented learning forms a significant substrate to other forms of learning, and that the ability to carry out other forms of learning widens behavioural (and therefore survival) options. The relative extent of those other forms of learning will depend on the extent to which the species has invested in brain development and other trappings of individual adaptation.

Levels of learning

This brings us to the question of levels of learning. Evolutionary development is not a matter of replacing one system with another. It occurs by adding systems, or modifying them for another purpose. Occasionally, something may become evolutionarily redundant, such as the human appendix. But for the most part, what has gone before remains, in one form or another. In the case of learning, there are basic forms of learning which relate directly to our evolutionary past; there are cognitive forms of learning which may have little or nothing to do with it; and there are any number of degrees of learning occurring between those two extremes.

If we explore the evolutionary history of the human brain, we find many psychological functions, including some forms of learning, mediated by structures which pre-date the cerebral cortex in evolutionary terms. At the most basic level, for example, we have pain avoidance, and indeed we find that pain-avoiding reflexes are not mediated by the brain at all, but by the spinal cord. The physiological correlates of the basic emotions of fear and anger are mediated by the medulla and brain stem; and those of relaxation and alertness by the pons and the midbrain. These are not unique to human beings: they are mammalian traits, shared by pretty well all mammals. The mechanism which we know by the name of classical conditioning is a form of learning which connects directly with this level of brain functioning.

More sophisticated emotions, and emotional memories, appear to be mediated by the limbic system, which also has direct connections with the olfactory system –a possible explanation for why smell, moods and mood-related memories so often appear to be closely linked. Sensory imagery and iconic representations are closely linked to the localised sensory areas of the cerebrum. But the cognitive aspects of memory, learning and problem-solving are much more diffused across the cerebral cortex, and harder to pin down in any systematic fashion, although brain scanning research does imply that different cognitive tasks do activate different areas of the so-called association cortex (for example, Posner *et al.*, 1988).

We are as yet a long way from being able to identify the way that more complex forms of learning are organised in the brain. But we do need to bear in mind that they, too, have an evolutionary history, and that this evolutionary history has shaped the way in which human cognitive processes operate. In particular, the fact that human beings have evolved as social animals has coloured our cognitions in a number of clearly identifiable ways, and probably several more that we have yet to identify.

The nature of human adaptation

The first thing that comes to mind when we consider the nature of human adaptation is that human beings live in so many different environments. We may have evolved initially in a tropical environment, although it is unlikely that the full evolutionary history of humankind occurred in just the one context. But modern humans spread across the globe pretty rapidly, and have shown an ability to cope with living in environments ranging from arctic conditions to tropical ones, and not forgetting the extreme seasonal variations experienced by those living in the centre of large continental land masses.

Infant sociability

Such a distribution of population would not have been possible if human beings had any sort of fixed behavioural adaptation to their environment. Survival skills which are helpful in tropical climates will quickly see you dead in arctic ones. Human adaptation is not about having inherited a tendency to produce specific behaviours. What we have inherited instead is a powerful tendency to learn from the other people around us.

From the moment a human infant is born, it responds more strongly to the stimulus of other people than it does to other aspects of its environments. It comes equipped with a range of behaviours, such as smiling in response to face-like stimuli, which render it likely to form reciprocal attachments with other human beings (Ahrens, 1954). And it responds particularly well to the kind of patterned, turn-taking interactions which form the basis of later communication, both verbal and non-verbal (Jaffe *et al.*, 1973).

Whether our tendency towards sociability is an outcome of the need to adapt to widely changing environments or whether our adaptability is an outcome of our sociability is one of those chicken-and-egg questions. But the fact remains that our capacity to adapt to such diverse environments is only possible because we are born with such strong social imperatives. Speaking globally, the only consistent thing in a human infant's experience is other people – stimuli from other sources are all variable, depending on climate and other aspects of the physical environment. But being so powerfully prepared to fix on, and learn from, other people means that the human infant can adapt to any environment that human beings live in.

Social functions of language

The acquisition of language – the human being's most distinctive asset – is one of those powerful social imperatives. Human language is far more than a purely cognitive process. It has powerful affiliative and interactive functions, which often override the cognitive components of linguistic communication (de Villiers and de Villiers, 1978). The Vygotskyan model of language development proposes that ontogenically, language and cognition begin as separate functions, and that the earliest function of language is affiliative and social; with its subsequent role in structuring cognition being a subsequent rather than a primary development (Vygotsky, 1962).

The differentiation between social-affiliative functions of language use and its syntactic and symbolic functions also continues in adult life. In any given social interaction, linguistic contributions are interpreted on several levels, not all of which are concerned with interpreting semantic content. A great deal of human linguistic activity serves primarily affiliative functions, to the extent that many everyday activities such as greeting exchanges, personal enquiries and verbal compliance have almost no semantic function.

Human learning is complex, and it is often difficult to identify specific periods during which a particular form of learning takes place. Attempts to do so, such as the Piagetian, have fallen foul of issues of social complexity and individual variability. There is some tentative evidence, however, that there are a few sensitive periods in human learning. The most well-known of these is concerned with language acquisition (for example, Lenneberg, 1967); but it is necessary to bear in mind that the idea that language acquisition occurs during a critical period had always been primarily theoretical, and is notably short of empirical verification. Nonetheless, there is an indication that the acquisition of a first language occurs most rapidly during childhood, although studies of severely deprived children do indicate that such learning can take place after puberty (Clarke and Clarke, 1976); and studies of the acquisition of a second language in adults have not dealt with total immersion learning, and are therefore not appropriate for true comparison.

Caveats aside, it is entirely appropriate that the human organism should be primed and ready to develop a function as essential to human survival and interaction as language. Human beings are powerfully prepared to learn language – so much so, that when the usual language acquisition channels are blocked, as in the case of deaf children, they will equally rapidly acquire a non-spoken language such as signing; and will use it with the same inventiveness and the same balance of semantic and affiliative functions as those using spoken languages.

There are a few indications of other types of sensitive period in the human being, and these too are concerned with social learning of one form or another. Many young social mammals 'school' during the period of growth equivalent to middle childhood – that is, they band together in same-age groups with fluid friendships. Human children appear to be no exception, and it may be that this, too, represents a sensitive period for some forms of social learning. The importance of same-sex and other-sex interactions during adolescence may be another example. These instances, however, are as yet speculative: although many researchers have been prepared to pronounce positively on the biological origins of various forms of human development, few of those same researchers have been prepared to collect systematic data on the matter from widely different human cultures, making it extremely difficult to distinguish between valid data and ideology.

As we've seen, studies of infant sociability show that the infant has a strong predisposition to respond to, and learn from, other people, in preference to other types of input. This preference is not restricted to infants. The predisposition to react more strongly to personal input from other people remains throughout childhood and in adult life. Conversations and personal contacts are more powerful forms of information input than those which operate through more detached or distant modes. We recognise this implicitly, in the way that we gather together to exchange ideas. In this information age, such gatherings should be entirely unnecessary. Yet the number of conferences, workshops and other such meetings is, if anything, increasing. A personal contact makes more of an impact on us than a written source, even though we may go to the written source for more detail or a more rigorous account.

Social learning, then, is a powerful mechanism, and a readiness to engage in it appears to be a lifelong characteristic of the human being. Many researchers have explored mechanisms of social learning: Stratton (1983) showed how human infants are particularly inclined to respond to transactions and contingencies resulting from social interaction; Bandura (1986) both stimulated and developed extensive research into imitation and modelling; and Tomasello *et al.* (1993) argued that the development of social learning in children mirrors the evolution of cultural learning as a whole. There is much more, of course: research into human social learning is extensive and wide-ranging. But the overall picture tells us a great deal about how prepared human beings are to learn from one another.

Human reasoning and social representations

Another instance of preparedness is indicated in the way that human beings go about abstract problem-solving. As Wason and others showed, human reasoning shows a number of characteristic forms of logical error (Wason and Johnson-Laird, 1972). But when such problems are contextualised, and seen in terms of everyday social experience, they appear less like errors and more like rational judgements. If I said, 'If it rains, I shall go to the cinema', and you met me at the cinema, you would be likely to conclude that it was raining. This would be an illogical conclusion, not warranted by my statement.

However, it would also be a perfectly rational conclusion, because your inference would have been informed by your social knowledge about human beings and about the way that we use language. You would be responding to what I meant, rather than what I said, and in such a situation, it would be perfectly reasonable to suppose that it was raining, since I wouldn't have been likely to be in the cinema otherwise. We are used to interpreting language in terms of our social knowledge, and there is considerable evidence about the way that our verbal recall is inaccurate in details, but remarkably accurate in terms of the gist, or social meaning, of what has been said (for example, Neisser, 1981).

Rationality and logicality are not the same in human thinking, because human thinking is overlaid by a social knowledge, which colours everything. The re-evaluations of Piagetian theory which have developed in recent years have resulted from the discovery that children can engage in much more complex forms of thinking than was previously thought possible at their age, as long as the problem is rooted in a familiar social context (Donaldson, 1978). We find some types of cognitive task much harder than others: we have difficulties dealing with decontextualised problems, with randomness (it is very difficult indeed for human beings to generate randomness, in almost any form –numbers, shapes and so on), with negatives (we take much longer to process negative information), and with infinity.

But we make hugely sophisticated judgements about social probability, recognise the social implications of group membership, and make inferences about social relationships very easily indeed. We also learn these things very early in life (Dunn, 1988). Our evolutionary history has left us well-prepared to handle information relevant to our survival, and in our particular case, that means social knowledge. But we are less ready to handle logic and abstract reasoning, and often can do so only after explicit training.

A further consequence of human social preparedness is the importance of shared social definitions of reality in human cognition. Consensus regarding the salience and implications of particular events or processes is achieved primarily through language, although it is also supplemented by and occasionally even expressed through non-verbal behaviour (Jodelet, 1991). This consensus results in social representations – cognitive constructions which connect directly with our sense of belonging to, and participating in, society.

Social representations are entirely different from the representations of reality which can be derived from direct experience, logic or individual reasoning. They are shaped by cultural and ideological values, transmitted and re-shaped through conversation. And they direct human responses to stimuli and events in particular directions (Moscovici, 1984). Two groups of people holding different social representations can become entirely incapable of communicating with one another: the same stimuli are interpreted entirely differently, and the shared definitions of reality held by members of each group become self-defining. Other socio-cognitive phenomena, such as groupthink (Janis, 1982), are directly related to the human tendency to develop shared social representations, and to apply these in preference to individual constructions of reality.

Human beings are particularly receptive to this type of social knowledge, and this receptivity is no accident. It is a direct consequence of the human being's evolution as a social animal, and of our preparedness to acquire social knowledge and socially defined knowledge in preference to almost any other kind. For most people, life is lived within an unchallenged cognitive framework of social consensus. Even people such as scientists, whose role is to challenge social consensus, or to enquire into it, locate their knowledge and ideas within a socially defined paradigm –a framework which is defined and accepted by the scientific community to which they belong.

Social identification

Since human survival relates to social participation and the utilisation of social knowledge, some levels of human learning bring us into dimensions of knowledge which are entirely different from simple, factual information. For example, an important aspect of our sociability is to do with 'belonging' to social groups. Sensitivity to group membership is universal, occurring in all human societies. It is a direct outcome of our evolution as social animals, which renders group membership particularly important. All human beings everywhere structure their social awareness in terms of various forms of 'them' and 'us'. Under specific circumstances, these become cognitively salient, and when they do, they colour, and sometimes even determine, the individual's cognitive appraisal of events and social stimuli. It is an interesting peripheral observation that this type of appraisal also remains in the Korsakoff's patient.

Any one human being may belong to numerous social groups, and may identify with any or all of them. This does not present cognitive difficulties, mainly because of the issue of salience. Group membership becomes cognitively relevant when the situation demands it, and remains in the background until that point. But an individual can switch from a purely personal identification to a social identification during a single conversation, if the social identity becomes salient. An argument about who does the washing-up, for example, can change rapidly from an interpersonal disagreement to a conflict between gender categories. Moreover, when a social identification has become salient, it brings into play its own set of associations, memories, arguments and knowledge, which may be quite different from the set of cognitions associated with a personal identity, or even with another social identity (Tajfel and Turner, 1979). This level of human cognition has often been overlooked, yet an awareness of its influence on cognitive appraisal and memory is vital for an understanding of human cognitive processes.

Levels of human learning

That is not to say, of course, that all human knowledge is purely social. On the contrary: there are a number of levels of human learning which both reflect our evolutionary history and allow us to transcend it. For example, human beings possess unconscious forms of memory which come into play at the most basic levels. Avoiding physical pain is a fundamental evolutionary imperative, and even an animal with a nervous system which is little more than a neural ladder, such as a flatworm, will learn to avoid pain-producing stimuli (Green, 1994). There is nothing cognitive about such learning: even human beings who have apparently lost all memory storage capacity, such as those with Korsakoff's syndrome, still learn to avoid painful stimuli.

In one well-known example, a Korsakoff's patient was pricked by a pin which a doctor had secreted in the palm of his hand, while shaking hands. The patient showed neither recall nor recognition on meeting the doctor the next day, but was nonetheless unwilling to shake hands. On being pressed to explain why, he speculated that sometimes people hid pins in their hands. He had no conscious memory of the event, and no recollection of having seen that individual before; but the experience of pain had nonetheless impressed itself into a memory which was apparently incapable of new information storage (Sacks, 1985).

Survival-oriented learning is a powerful substrate to other types of learning. In humans, this substrate operates at such basic levels that it is often entirely unconscious. Not all learning occurs at the conscious, cerebral level (Seligman, 1971). Yet these lower forms of learning can also shape, and structure, cognitions. Bower, for example, showed how a person's mood directly affects what they are able to recall. In an experimental intervention, people who experienced an inducted negative mood showed increased recall of negatively valenced memories, and decreased recall of positive events. When they were put in a positive mood, the outcome was reversed (Bower, 1981).

Human beings are also able to engage in abstract forms of thought, even if they do tend to make logical errors. There is some cross-cultural evidence that the active exercising of this facility may also be universal, although it takes different forms in different cultures. The use of riddles, word-games and mathematical puzzles are common ways of educating the young in non-technological societies, and they help to train a capacity for decontextualised thinking. This type of learning has to be taught by adults, and is not picked up as automatically as social knowledge.

The fact that such learning is not picked up as readily as social knowledge, of course, conveys its own message. But humans are capable of acquiring this knowledge, and it has a place in our understanding of human cognition. We need to be wary, though, of models of human cognition which consider it to be the only type of knowledge that matters. Our challenge lies in understanding the interaction between social and abstract knowledge in human thinking, and in recognising the degree to which social forms of knowledge shape and influence cognitive appraisal.

In modelling human cognitive architecture, therefore, we need to be aware that it occurs within a social matrix which is far more than a simple set of data inputs. Pre-adaptation of the human being towards social stimuli even from infancy, the social dimensions of language, and the role of social representations and group membership in shaping appraisal and response are fundamental characteristics of human cognition. The social matrix shapes, directs and colours human cognition, and needs to be treated as fundamental if effective cognitive modelling is to be achieved.

Afterword

In this book, I have tried to show how patterns of thinking have emerged within the psychological discipline, and how they exert their influences on subsequent generations. Very often, that has meant presenting ideas in their historical context: if we are truly to understand psychology's current concerns and conflicts, we also need to understand its history and the social movements which have shaped that history.

In the fourteen essays of this book, I have challenged many of the psychological manifestations of reductionist and repressive thinking which are, or have been, apparent in psychological research and argument. Those challenges have been made both on scientific and on ideological grounds. At the same time, I have tried to present some of the alternatives: to criticise without presenting alternatives is a sterile exercise, in my view. I have tried to show how these psychological arguments have been shaped by wider social developments, and in turn contributed to accepted social beliefs – and not always in positive ways.

Sometimes, these arguments have dealt with issues which are distasteful, or which some psychologists would prefer to wipe from our history. But that is unrealistic. As scientists, we cannot evade our social responsibilities by turning away from some of the less palatable truths about our history. Rather, we need to be fully aware of the social implications of what we are doing and what our predecessors have done. Only in that way can we build a positive psychology, which can work towards furthering our human potential.

NICKY HAYES

Glossary

Agency theory	The idea that people operate most effectively when they are active in making their own decisions about their lives, and in carrying those decisions through.
angular gyrus	A part of the cerebral cortex of the brain which mediates reading, receiving information from the visual cortex and converting it to the equivalent of spoken language.
associationism	The idea that all human knowledge derives from associating one small item of information with another.
attribution theory	A theory which is concerned with the reasons that people give for why things happen.
autism	An emotional disorder in which the person is withdrawn and unable to interact effectively with other people, which may arise from the lack of a 'theory of mind'.
behaviourism	A reductionist approach to psychology which assumed that overt behaviour was the only possible or desirable subject of interest for psychologists, and that all behaviour would eventually be reduced down to links between stimulus and response.
biological determinism	The idea that human behaviour is entirely caused by our biology.
Cartesian dualism	Descartes's idea that the mind and body are distinct and separate.
closure	The Gestalt principle of perception according to which we tend to perceive complete, 'closed' objects rather than incomplete ones, even when the information we are receiving is incomplete.
cognitive psychology	The branch of psychology which is concerned with understanding how the mind works and how we process information.

covariance theory   The version of attribution theory which explains the reasons that we give for why things happen, as the result of variation in consensus, consistency and distinctiveness.

deindividuation   An approach to explaining crowd behaviour by arguing that the anonymity of belonging to a crowd results in people behaving in a less inhibited and more impulsive fashion.

dualism   *See* Cartesian dualism.

dyslexia   In its strictest form, a brain disorder in which reading or the perception of letters is abnormal. Also used more widely as a rationalisation to justify bad spelling.

empiricism   An approach to understanding the world which assumes that only information which can be detected physically and measured should count as valid knowledge.

epistemology   The study of what counts as knowledge, or as 'real' information.

ethogenics   An approach to studying human social interaction which emphasises the value of people's accounts of their experience, and of the episode as the basic social unit.

ethological   To do with studying behaviour in its natural environment.

eugenics   An elitist theory of human nature which proposes that those with 'inferior' genes should be prevented from breeding so that those who are supposedly 'superior' will pass on their genes and so improve the human race. Eugenics was the basis for the Nazi concentration camps and the American sterilisation laws.

existentialist   A philosophical approach which emphasises the individual's responsibility for their own existence in the world.

genetic reductionism   The somewhat naïve and sometimes dangerous belief that all human behaviour will eventually be understood simply as the product of genetic influences.

genotype	The genetic code contained in DNA sequences within the cell nucleus of the body, which spells out how the organism will grow and develop, physically, in the appropriate environment.
Gestalt psychology	A school of psychology which opposed the stimulus–response (S–R) reductionism of the behaviourists and instead emphasised a human tendency towards wholeness of experience and cognition.
hereditarian	A type of theory which emphasises inherited mechanisms (for example, in intelligence) to the exclusion, or minimisation, of other factors.
hermeneutics	The study of the nature of social meaning and interpretation of human experience.
humanism	A school of thought which emphasises the positive aspects of human nature, and sees human potential as a reservoir of potentially positive energies.
interactionism	The approach to understanding human and animal behaviour which emphasises links between different levels of explanation, and is therefore the opposite of reductionism.
introspectionism	An approach to study which uses the method of looking 'inwards' to analyse or explore one's own mental state, beliefs or ideas.
libido	The sexual and life-affirming energy which Freud initially saw as the energising factor for all human behaviour. In later work, he added the idea of a destructive energy: thanatos.
Mendelian genetics	The generally accepted approach to genetic mechanisms, in which genetic transmission is seen as occurring at conception, by the combination of genes and chromosomes from the parents, with no further adjustments to or development of the genes throughout the organism's lifetime.
miscegenation	The Nazi idea that the human race would be weakened by breeding those with supposedly 'superior' genes with those with supposedly 'inferior' genes – an idea based on eugenics.

nativism	An approach which assumes that knowledge or abilities are innate, and will develop with maturity without having to be specially trained or taught.
neurological reductionism	The belief that all human behaviour will eventually be understood as nothing but the action of nerve cells in the brain or spinal cord.
personal construct theory	An approach which emphasises the individual ways that people make sense of, or construe, their social and personal worlds.
phenotype	The physical characteristics which an individual develops as evidence of the interaction between their genes and the environment in which they have developed.
pheromones	Chemicals which are released into the air by animals which, when received by another animal, exert a direct influence on its hormonal system and sometimes its behaviour.
phylogenetic	To do with the sequence of evolutionary changes through which a particular species or set of species has passed.
Popperian	Deriving from the theories of the philosopher of science Karl Popper.
psychoanalytic	To do with, or deriving from, the approach known as psychoanalysis, in which the aim is to analyse the unconscious mind with a view to identifying hidden meanings and motives.
reductionism	An approach to understanding behaviour which focuses on one single level of explanation and ignores others. The opposite of interactionism.
relativism	An approach to understanding the world which avoids value judgements and takes all frameworks or perspectives as having equal value.
schizophrenia	A mental disorder in which the person experiences a separation or split from reality.
social cognition	The way that we think about and interpret social information and social experience.

social identity theory	A theory which emphasises how membership of social groups forms a significant part of the self-concept, such that people sometimes respond primarily as group members and not as individuals.
social impact theory	A reductionist approach to understanding social phenomena which adds up relevant factors like the number of people present and their importance to the individual concerned.
social reductionism	An approach to understanding human behaviour which argues that human social behaviour can be understood purely in terms of individual characteristics and qualities.
social representation theory	A theory which looks at how shared beliefs develop and are transmitted among social groups, and how they serve an important function in explaining reality and in justifying social action.
sociobiology	A reductionist approach to explaining animal behaviour, sometimes applied to humans, which argues that all behaviour is driven by units of survival referred to as 'genes' (not the same as the biological concept), and that individuals and species are nothing but mechanisms by which these 'genes' can perpetuate themselves.
S–R	The common abbreviation for stimulus–response. S–R connections were considered to be the basic element in all learning by the behaviourists.
thanatos	The negative, destructive energy proposed by Freud as a counterpart for the positive sexual energy known as libido, and invoked in order to explain the destruction and carnage of the First World War in psychoanalytic terms.
theory of mind	An awareness that other people can have a systematic set of thoughts, feelings and memories which are not the same as one's own.
Wernicke's area	An area of the cerebral cortex which, when damaged, produces problems in comprehending verbal information.
Zeitgeist	The spirit or mood of the times.

References

Abelson, R. P. (1976) 'Script processing in attitude formation and decision making', in J. S. Carroll and J. W. Payne (eds), *Cognition and Social Behaviour*. Hillsdale, NJ: Erlbaum.

Adorno, T. W., Frenkel-Brunswik, G., Levinson, D. J. and Sanford, R. N. (1950) *The Authoritarian Personality*. New York: Harper.

Ahrens, S. R. (1954) 'Beitrage zur Entwicklung des Physiognomie und Mimikerkennes' (Contributions on the development of physiognomy and mimicry recognition), *Zeitschrift für Experimentelle und Angewandte Psychologie*, 2: 412–54.

Allport, F. H. (1924) *Social Psychology*. Boston Mass.: Houghton-Mifflin.

Annis, R. C. and Frost, B. (1973) 'Human visual ecology and orientation antistropies in acuity', *Science* (182): 729–31.

Appleby, M. (1985) 'Hawks, doves...and chickens', *New Scientist*, 10 January 1985, 16–18.

Ardrey, R. (1966) *The Territorial Imperative*. New York: Dell.

Arendt, H. (1963) *Eichmann in Jerusalem: A Report on the Banality of Evil*. New York: Viking Press.

Argyle, M. and Crossland, J. (1987) 'The dimensions of positive emotions', *British Journal of Social Psychology*, 26: 127–37.

Asch, S. E. (1956) 'Studies of independence and conformity: a minority of one against a unanimous majority', *Psychological Monographs*, 70(9).

Baddeley, A. D. (1983) 'Working memory', *Philosophical Translations of the Royal Society of London B(302)* 311–24.

Bandura, A. (1986) *Social Foundations of Thought and Action: A Social Cognitive Theory*. Englewood Cliffs, NJ: Prentice-Hall.

Bannister, D. and Fransella, F. (1971), *Inquiring man: the theory of personal constructs*, Harmondsworth: Penguin.

Banyard, P. (1989) 'Hillsborough', *Psychology News*, 2(7): 4–9.

Banyard, P. (1991, 1992, 1993 etc.) Personal communication.

Bard, D. and Sachs, J. (1977) Language acquisition patterns in two normal children of deaf patterns. Paper presented to the Second Annual Boston University Conference on Language Acquisition October 1977. Cited in de Villiers, J. G. and de Villiers, P. A. (1978) *Early Language*. London: Fontana.

Bartlett, F. C. (1932) *Remembering*. London: Cambridge University Press.

Bateson, G., Jackson, D., Haley, J. and Weakland, J. (1956) 'Towards a theory of schizophrenia', *Behavioural Science*, 4: 251–64.

Baumrind, D. (1964) 'Some thoughts on the ethics of research: after reading Milgram's study of obedience', *American Psychologist*, 19: 421–3.

Benewick, R. and Holton, R. (1987) 'The peaceful crowd: crowd solidarity and the Pope's visit to Britain', in G. Gaskell and R. Benewick (eds), *The Crowd in Contemporary Britain*. London: Sage.

Bettelheim, B. (1943) 'Individual and mass behaviour in extreme situations', *Journal of Abnormal and Social Psychology*, 38: 417–52.

Blakemore, C. (1984) 'The sensory worlds of animals and man', address delivered to the Annual Meeting of the Association for the Teaching of Psychology, London, 1984.

Blakemore, C. and Cooper, J. F. (1970) 'Development of the brain depends on the visual environment' *Nature*, 228: 477–8.

Bower, G. H. (1981) 'Mood and memory', *American Psychologist*, 36: 129–48.

British Psychological Society (1981) 'Principles governing the employment of psychological tests', *Bulletin of the British Psychological Society*, 34: 317–18.

British Psychological Society (1985) 'Guidelines for the use of animals in research', *Bulletin of the British Psychological Society*, 38: 289–91.

British Psychological Society (1990) 'Revised ethical principles for research with human subjects', *The Psychologist*, 3: 269–72.

Brown, G. W. and Harris, T. (1978) *The Social Origins of Depression: A Study in Psychiatric Disorder in Women*. London: Tavistock.

Bruner, J. S. (1973) *Beyond the Information Given: Studies in the Psychology of Knowing*. New York: W. W. Norton.

Burt, C. (1955) 'The evidence for the concept of intelligence', *British Journal of Educational Psychology*, 25: 158–77.

Burt, C. (1966) 'The genetic determination of differences in intelligence: a study of monozygotic twins reared together and apart', *British Journal of Psychology*, 57: 137–53.

Chomsky, N. (1959) 'Review of Skinner's "verbal behaviour"', *Language*, 35: 26–58.

Clarke, A. M. and Clarke, A. D. B. (1976) *Early Experience: Myth and Evidence*. London: Open Books.

Davies, G., Haworth, G. and Hirschler, S. (1992) 'Ethics in psychological research: guidelines for students at pre-degree levels', *Psychology Teaching: Journal of the Association for the Teaching of Psychology*, 1: 4–10.

Dawkins, R. (1976) *The Selfish Gene*. Harmondsworth: Penguin.

de Villiers, J. G. and de Villiers, P. A. (1978) *Early Language*. London: Fontana.

De Waal, F. B. M. (1989) *Peacemaking among Primates*. Cambridge, Mass.: Harvard University Press.

Descartes, R. (1637) *Dioptrics*.

Descartes, R. (1641) *Meditations on the First Philosophy*.

Di Giacomo, J. P. (1980) 'Intergroup alliances and rejections within a protest movement (analysis of the social representations)', *European Journal of Social Psychology*, 10: 329–44.

Doise, W. (1984) 'Social representations, inter-group experiments and levels of analysis', in R. M. Farr and S. Moscovici (eds), *Social Representations*. Cambridge: Cambridge University Press.

Doise, W., Deschamps, J.-C. and Meyer, G. (1978) 'The accentuation of intra-category similarities', in H. Tajfel (ed.), *Differentiation between Social Groups*. London: Academic Press.

Dollard, J. and Miller, N. E. (1950) *Personality and Psychotherapy: An Analysis in Terms of Learning, Thinking and Culture*. New York: McGraw-Hill.

Donaldson, M. (1978) *Children's Minds*. London: Fontana/Collins.

Duck, S. (1988) *Relating to Others*. Milton Keynes: Open University Press.

Dunn, J. (1988) The Beginnings of Social Understanding. Oxford: Blackwell.

Ebbinghaus, H. (1885) *Memory: A Contribution to Experimental Psychology* (reprinted 1964) New York: Dover.

Edwards, G. and Owens, G. (1984) 'The clinical ecology debate: some issues arising', *Bulletin of the British Psychological Society*, 37: 325–8.

Evans, J. St. B. T., Newstead, S. E. and Byrne, R. M. J. (1993) *Human Reasoning: The Psychology of Deduction*. Hove: Lawrence Erlbaum Associates.

Eysenck, H. J. (1947) *Dimensions of Personality*. London: Routledge.

Farr, R. M. (1984) 'Social representations: their role in the design and execution of laboratory experiments', in R. M. Farr and S. Moscovici (eds), *Social Representations*. Cambridge: Cambridge University Press.

Felipe, N. J. and Sommer, R. (1966) 'Invasion of personal space', *Social Problems*, 14: 206–14.

Festinger, L., Riecken, H. W. and Schachter, S. (1956) *When Prophecy Fails*. Minneapolis: University of Minneapolis Press.

Fischler, C. (1980) 'Food habits, social change and the nature/culture dilemma', *Social Science Information*, 19: 937–53.

Fisher, A. E. (1964) 'Chemical stimulation of the brain', *Scientific American*, 210(6): 60–8.

Freud, S. (1901) 'The psychopathology of everyday life', republished 1953 in J. Strachey (ed.), *The Standard Edition of the Complete Psychological Works of Sigmund Freud, Vol. 6*. London: Hogarth.

Freud, S. (1920) *Beyond the Pleasure Principle* (1975 edn) New York: Norton.

Galton, F. (1869) 'Classification of men according to their natural gifts', in J. J. Jenkins and D. G. Paterson (eds) (1961) *Studies in Individual Differences*. New York: Appleton-Century-Croft.

Galton, F. (1884) *Hereditary Genius*. New York: Appleton.

Gamson, W. B., Fireman, B. and Rytina, S. (1982) *Encounters with Unjust Authority*. Homewood, Ill.: Dorsey Press.

Gardner, R. A. and Gardner, B. T. (1969) 'Teaching sign language to a chimpanzee', *Science*, 165: 664–72.

Gesell, A. (1929) 'Maturation and infant behaviour patterns', *Psychological Review*, 36: 307–19.

Gibson, J. J. (1979) *The Ecological Approach to Visual Perception*. Boston Mass.: Houghton Mifflin.

Goddard, H. H. (1912) *The Kallikak Family: A Study in the Heredity of Feeble-mindedness*. New York: Macmillan.

Gould, J. L. and Marler, P. R. (1987) 'Learning by instinct', *Scientific American*, 256(1): 62–74.

Gould, S. J. (1978) *Ever since Darwin: Reflections in Natural History*. Harmondsworth: Penguin.

Gould, S. J. (1981) *The Mismeasure of Man*. Harmondsworth: Penguin.

Gray, J. A. (1985) 'A whole and its parts: behaviour, the brain, cognition and emotion', *Bulletin of the British Psychological Society*, 38: 99–112.

Green, S. (1994) *Principles of Biopsychology*. Hove: Lawrence Erlbaum Associates.

Gregory, R. L. (1966) *Eye and Brain*. New York: McGraw-Hill.

Gregory, R. L. (1973) 'The confounded eye', in R. L. Gregory and E. H. Gombrich (eds), *Illusion in Nature and Art*. London: Duckworth.

Hailman, J. P. (1969) 'How an instinct is learned', *Scientific American*, 221(6): 98–106.

Harlow, H. F. (1949) 'The formation of learning sets', *Psychological Review* 56: 51–65.

Harlow, H. F. (1959) 'Love in infant monkeys', *Scientific American*, 200: 64–74.

Harlow, H. F., and Harlow, M. K. (1949) 'Learning to think', *Scientific American Offprints*, no. 415. New York: W. H. Freeman & Co.

Harlow, H. F., and Harlow, M. K. (1962) 'Social deprivation in monkeys', *Scientific American*, 207(5): 136–46.

Harré, R. (1979) *Social Being*. Oxford: Blackwell.

Harris, P. L. (1988) *Children and Emotion: The Development of Psychological Understanding*. Oxford: Blackwell.

Harris, P. L., Donnelly, K., Guz, G. R. and Pitt-Watson, R. (1986) Children's understanding of the distinction between real and apparent emotion, *Child Development*, 57: 895–909.

Hay, D. and Morisey, A. (1978) 'Reports of ecstatic, paranormal or religious experience in Great Britain and the United States: a comparison of trends', *Journal for the Scientific Study of Religion*, 17: 255–68.

Hayes, N. J. (1991) 'Social identity, social representations and organisational culture', unpublished PhD thesis, CNAA/Huddersfield Polytechnic.

Hayes, N. J. (1997) 'Theory-led thematic analysis: social identification in small companies', in N. Hayes (ed.), *Introduction to Qualitative Analysis in Psychology*. Hove: Lawrence Erlbaum Associates.

Hebb, D. O. (1949) *The Organisation of Behaviour*. New York: Wiley.

Hess, E. H. (1972) '"Imprinting" in a natural laboratory', *Scientific American*, 227(2): 24–31.

Hinde, R. A. (1987) *Individuals, Relationships and Culture*. Cambridge: Cambridge University Press.

Hobbes, T. (1651) *Leviathan*. London: Everyman, 1914.

Hogg, M. A. and Abrams, D. (1988) *Social Identifications: A Social Psychology of Intergroup Relations and Group Processes*. London: Routledge.

Horton, R. (1967) 'African traditional thought and Western science', in M. F. D. Young (ed.) (1971) *Knowledge and Control*. Cambridge, Mass.: Addison-Wesley.

Hubel, D. H. (1979) 'The brain', *Scientific American*, **214**(3): 44–53.

Jaffe, J., Stern, D. L. and Peery, J. C. (1973) '"Conversational" complexity of gaze behaviour in pre-linguistic human development', *Journal of Psycholinguistic Research*, **2**: 321–30.

James, W. (1890) *Principles of Psychology*. New York: Holt.

Janis, I. L. (1982) *Groupthink: Psychological Studies of Policy Decisions and Fiascos*. Boston Mass.: Houghton Mifflin.

Jensen, A. R. (1969) 'How much can we boost IQ and scholastic achievement?', *Harvard Educational Review*, **33**: 1–123.

Jodelet, D. (1984) 'The representation of the body and its transformations', in R. M. Farr and S. Moscovici (eds), *Social Representations*. Cambridge: Cambridge University Press.

Jodelet, D. (1991) *Madness and Social Representations*. London: Harvester Wheatsheaf.

Jones, E. E. and Sigall, H. (1971) 'The bogus pipeline: a new paradigm for measuring affect and attitude', *Psychological Bulletin*, **76**: 349–64.

Jung, C. (1961) *Memories, Dreams, Reflections*. London: Random House.

Kallmann, F. J. (1938) *The Genetics of Schizophrenia*. New York: J. J. Augustin.

Kamin, L. J. (1974) *The Science and Politics of IQ*. Potomac, Md: Lawrence Erlbaum Associates.

Kelley, H. H. (1973) 'The process of causal attribution', *American Psychologist*, **28**: 107–28.

Kelly, G. A. (1955) *The Psychology of Personal Constructs*. New York: W. W. Norton.

Köhler, W. (1925) *The Mentality of Apes*. New York: Harcourt Brace.

Kruglanski, A. W. (1980); 'Lay epistemo-logic, process and contents: another look at attribution theory', *Psychological Review*, **87**: 70–87.

Kuhn, T. S. (1962) *The Structure of Scientific Revolutions*. Chicago, ill.: Chicago University Press.

Laing, R. D. (1965) *The Divided Self*. Harmondsworth: Penguin.

Laing, R. D. and Esterson, G. S. (1968) *Sanity, Madness and the Family*. Harmondsworth: Penguin.

Lalljee, M. (1981) 'Attribution theory and the analysis of explanations', in C. Antaki (ed.), *The Psychology of Ordinary Explanations of Social Behaviour*. London: Academic Press.

Latané, B. (1981) 'The psychology of social impact', *American Psychologist*, **36**: 343–56.

Le Bon, G. (1895) *The Crowd: A Study of the Popular Mind*. New York: Viking Press.

Leeper, R. (1935) 'A study of a neglected portion of the field of learning – the development of sensory organisation', *Journal of Genetic Psychology*, **46**: 41–75.

Lenneberg, G. H. (1967) *Biological Foundations of Language*. New York: Wiley.

Locke, J. (1700) *An Essay Concerning Human Understanding*, 4th edn (republished 1959). New York: Dover.

Loftus, G. R. and Loftus, E. F. (1975) *Human Memory: The Processing of Information*. New York: Halsted Press.

Lorenz, K. (1950) 'The comparative method in studying innate behaviour patterns', *Symposium of the Society of Experimental Biology*, **4**: 221–68.

Lorenz, K. (1966) *On Aggression*. New York: Harcourt Brace & World.

Lutz, C. A. (1990) 'Morality, domination and understandings of "justifiable anger" among the Ifaluk', in G. R. Semin and K. J. Gergen (eds), *Everyday Understanding: Social and Scientific Implications*. London: Sage.

March, P., Rosser, E. and Harré, R. (1978) *The Rules of Disorder*. London: Routledge.

Marler, P. R. (1982) 'Avian and primate communication: the problem of natural categories', *Neuroscience & Biobehavioural Reviews*, **6**: 87–94.

Marler, P. R. and Tamura, M. (1964) 'Culturally transmitted patterns of vocal behaviour in sparrows', *Science*, **146**: 1483–6.

Marshall, J. R. (1984) 'The genetics of schizophrenia revisited', *Bulletin of the British Psychological Society*, **37**: 177–81.

Maslow, A. H. (1954) *Motivation and Personality*. New York: Harper & Row.

McDougall, W. (1920) *The Group Mind: A Sketch of the Principles of Collective Psychology with Some Attempt to Apply Them to the Interpretation of National Life and Character*. Cambridge: Cambridge University Press.

McNicholas, J. and Collis, G. M. (2000) 'Dogs as catalysts for social interactions: robustness of the effect', *British Journal of Psychology*, **91**: 61–70.

Milgram, S. (1963) 'Behavioural study of obedience', *Journal of Abnormal Psychology*, **67**: 371–8.

Milgram, S. (1973) *Obedience to authority*. London: Tavistock.

Morris, D. (1967) *The Naked Ape*. London: Cape.

Morris, P. E., Gruneberg, M. M., Sykes, R. N. and Merrick, A. (1981) 'Football knowledge and the acquisition of new results', *British Journal of Psychology*, **72**: 479–83.

Moscovici, S. (1961) *La psychoanalyse: son image et son public*. Paris: Presses Universitaires de France.

Moscovici, S. (1984) 'The phenomenon of social representations', in R. M. Farr and S. Moscovici (eds), *Social Representations*. Cambridge: Cambridge University Press.

Moscovici, S. and Hewstone, M. (1983) 'Social representations: from the "naive" to the "amateur" scientist', in M. Hewstone (ed.) *Attribution Theory: Social and Functional Extensions*. Oxford: Blackwell.

Neisser, U. (1976) *Cognition and Reality: Principles and Implications of Cognitive Psychology*. San Francisco: W. H. Freeman.

Neisser, U. (1981) 'John Dean's memory: a case study', *Cognition*, 9: 1–22.

Neisser, U. (1982) *Memory Observed: Remembering in Natural Contexts*. San Francisco: W. H. Freeman & Co.

Newman, H. H., Freeman, F. N. and Holzinger, K. J. (1937) *Twins: A Study of Heredity and Environment*. Chicago, ill.: University of Chicago Press.

Orne, M. T. (1962) 'On the social psychology of the psychological experiment: with particular reference to demand characteristics and their implications', *American Psychologist*, 17: 276–83.

Paine, T. (1791) *The Rights of Man*. London: Freethought Publishing Co.

Perrin, S. and Spencer, C. (1980) 'The Asch effect: a child of its times?', *Bulletin of the British Psychological Society*, 32: 405–6.

Piaget, J. (1952) *The Origins of Intelligence in Children*. New York: International Universities Press.

Posner, M. L., Petersen, S. E., Fox, P. T. and Raichle, M. E. (1988) 'Localisation of cognitive operations in the human brain', *Science*, 240: 1627–31.

Reynolds, P. D. (1982) 'Moral judgements: strategies for analysis with application to covert participant observation', in M. Bulmer (ed.), *Social Research Ethics*. London: Macmillan.

Rippere, V. (1988) 'Introducing clinical ecology', *Psychology News*, 2(4): 4–8.

Rippere, V. and Adams, R. (1982) 'Clinical ecology and why clinical psychology needs it', *Bulletin of the British Psychological Society*, 35: 151–2.

Rogers, C. R. (1961) *On Becoming a Person: A Therapist's View of Psychotherapy*. London: Constable.

Rose, S. (1984) 'Sociobiology: the total synthesis', in S. Rose, L. Kamin and R. Lewontin, *Not in Our Genes*. Harmondsworth: Penguin.

Rose, S. (1992) *The Making of Memory: From Molecules to Mind*. London: Bantam Press.

Rose, S., Kamin, L. and Lewontin, R. (1984) *Not in Our Genes*. Harmondsworth: Penguin.

Rosenhan, D. L. (1973) 'On being sane in insane places', *Science*, 179: 250–8.

Rosenthal, R. and Fode, K. L. (1963) 'The effect of experimenter bias on the performance of the albino rat', *Behavioural Science*, 8: 183–9.

Rosenthal, R. and Jacobsen, L. (1968) *Pygmalion in the Classroom: Teacher Expectations and Pupil Intellectual Development*. New York: Holt, Rinehart & Winston.

Rosenzweig, M. R. and Bennett, E. L. (1976) 'Enriched environments: facts, factors and fantasies' in J. L. McGaugh and L. Petrinovitch (eds), *Knowing, Thinking and Believing*. New York: Plenum.

Rotter, J. B. (1966) 'Generalised expectancies for internal vs external control of reinforcement', *Psychological Monographs*, 80(1).

Rumbaugh, D. M. (1977) *Language Learning by a Chimpanzee: The Lana Project*. New York: Academic Press.

Rutter, M. (1981) *Maternal Deprivation Reassessed*, 2nd edn. Harmondsworth: Penguin.

Sacks, O. (1985) *The Man Who Mistook His Wife for a Hat*. London: Picador.

Schank, R. and Abelson, R. (1977) *Scripts, Plans, Goals and Understanding: An Enquiry into Human Knowledge*. Hillsdale, NJ: Erlbaum.

Seligman, M. E. P. (1970) 'On the generality of the laws of learning', *Psychological Review* 77: 406–418.

Seligman, M. E. P. (1971) 'Phobias and preparedness', *Behaviour Therapy* 2: 307–20.

Shayer, M. and Adey, P. (1981) *Towards a Science of Science Teaching*. London: Heinemann.

Sherif, M. (1936) *The Psychology of Social Norms*. New York: Harper & Bros.

Silverman, I. (1977) *The Human Subject in the Psychological Laboratory*. New York: Pergamon.

Singer, P. (1976) *Animal liberation*. London: Cape.

Skinner, B. F. (1953) *Science and Human Behavior*. New York: Macmillan.

Skinner, B. F. (1957) *Verbal behaviour*. New York: Appleton-Century-Crofts.

Skinner, B. F. (1972) *Beyond Freedom and Dignity*. Harmondsworth: Penguin.

Sluckin, W. (1964) *Imprinting and Early Learning*. London: Methuen.

Smyth, M. M., Morris, P. E., Levy, P. and Ellis, A. W. (1987) *Cognition in Action*. London: Lawrence Erlbaum.

Spears, R. and Manstead, A. S. (1989) 'The social context of stereotyping and differentiation', *European Journal of Social Psychology*, **19**: 101–21.

Spencer, H. (1884) *The Man versus the State*. Harmondsworth: Pelican Classics.

Sternberg, R. J. (1987) *The Triangle of Love*. New York: Basic Books.

Stratton, P. M. (1983) 'Biological preprogramming of infant behaviour', *Journal of Child Psychology and Psychiatry*, **24**(2): 301–9.

Stratton, P. M. and Swaffer, R. (1988) 'Maternal causal beliefs for abused and handicapped children', *Journal of Reproductive and Infant Psychology*, **6**: 201–16.

Tajfel, H. (1972) 'Some developments in European social psychology', *European Journal of Social Psychology*, **2**: 307–22.

Tajfel, H. (1981) *Human Groups and Social Categories: Studies in Social Psychology*. Cambridge: Cambridge University Press.

Tajfel, H. and Turner, J. C. (1979) 'An integrative theory of intergroup conflict', in W. G. Austin and S. Worchel (eds), *The Social Psychology of Intergroup Relations*. Monterey, Calif. Brooks/Cole.

Tajfel, H. and Wilkes, A. L. (1963) 'Classification and quantitative judgement', *British Journal of Psychology*, **54**: 101–14.

Taylor, D. M. and Jaggi, V. (1974) 'Ethnocentrism and causal attribution in a S. Indian context', *Journal of Cross-Cultural Psychology*, **5**: 162–71.

Terrace, H. S. (1979) *Nim*. New York: Knopf.

Tinbergen, N. (1951) *The Study of Instinct*. Oxford: Oxford University Press.

Tolman, E. C. (1932) *Purposive Behaviour in Animals and Man*. New York: Century.

Tomasello, M., Kruger, A. and Ratner, H. (1993) 'Cultural learning', *Behavioural and Brain Sciences*, 16: 495–552.

Vygotsky, L. S. (1962) *Thought and Language*. Cambridge, Mass.: MIT Press.

Walster, E. (1965) 'The effects of self-esteem on romantic liking,' *Journal of Experimental Social Psychology*, 1: 184–97.

Wason, P. C. and Johnson-Laird, P. N. (1972) *Psychology of Reasoning: Structure and Content*. Cambridge, Mass.: Harvard University Press.

Watson, J. B. (1913) 'Psychology from the standpoint of a behaviourist', *Psychological Review*, 20: 158–77.

Watson, J. B. (1924) *Behaviourism*. New York: J. B. Lippincott.

Watson, J. B. and Rayner, R. (1920) 'Conditioned emotional reactions', *Journal of Experimental Psychology*, 3: 1–14.

Whittaker, E. M. (1982) 'Dyslexia and the flat earth', *Bulletin of the British Psychological Society*, 35: 97–9.

Wilson, E. O. (1975) *Sociobiology: The New Synthesis*. Cambridge, Mass.: Harvard University Press.

Wilson, E. O. (1978) *On Human Nature*. Cambridge, Mass.: Harvard University Press.

Wimmer, H., Gruber, S. and Perner, J. (1984) Young children's conception of lying: conceptual realism-moral subjectivism, *Journal of Experimental Child Psychology*, 37: 1–30.

Wimmer, H. and Perner J. (1983) Beliefs about beliefs: representations and constraining function of wrong beliefs in young children's understanding of deception *Cognition*, 13: 103–28.

Wolpe, J. (1958) *Psychotherapy by Reciprocal Inhibition*. Stanford, Calif.: Stanford University Press.

Wundt, W. (1905) *Grundriss der Psychologie*. Leipzig: Engelmann.

Zimbardo, P. G. (1969) 'The human choice: individuation, reason and order versus deindividuation, impulse and chaos', in W. J. Arnold and D. Levine (eds), *Nebraska Symposium on Motivation 17*. Lincoln: University of Nebraska Press.

Index

Weakland, J.   *see* Bateson, G. *et al.*
Whittaker, E. M.   142
Wilkes, A. L.   *see* Tajfel, H. and
     Wilkes, A. L.
Wilson, E. O.   11–12, 155–60,
     162–3, 171
Wimmer, H., Gruber, S. and
     Perner, J.   101

Wimmer, H. and Perner, J.   100
Wolpe, J.   24
working mothers   66
Wundt, W.   4, 19, 83, 106

Zimbardo, P. G.   14, 73, 82–3
zone of proximal development
     (ZPD)   103–4